"Bob Losyk's book, *Get a Grip!*, is exactly what the doctor ordered: finally, a book that's easy to read and gives you choices in combating the real killer, stress."

—Carl C. Thompson, Executive
Director, Society of Government
Meeting Professionals

"This book provides the antidote to a chronic killer in the workplace. Up-to-date information and practical tips, mixed with motivation for survivors. Highly recommended!"

—Dianna Booher, *Speak with
Confidence: Powerful Presentations
That Inform, Inspire, and Persuade*

"Bob Losyk's book, *Get a Grip!*, can help you identify whether you are a candidate for burnout. More importantly, Bob provides proven solutions for effectively coping with workplace stress. You owe it to yourself, your family, and your co-workers to read *Get a Grip!*"

—Don Wilson, President and CEO,
Association of Small Business
Development Centers

"*Get a Grip!* is filled with practical steps and techniques for de-stressing your life and getting the most out of every day. A must-read for anyone who wants to thrive in the twenty-first century."

—Daniel Burrus, *Technotrends*

"*Get a Grip!* is a book everyone should read in these fast-paced, highly stressful times. It's a reader friendly book, filled with usable, practical advice for eliminating stress for everyone in all walks of life."

—Dr. Tony Alessandra,
The Platinum Rule

"Just in time! Stress! Life-work balance is out of balance! It's time to *Get a Grip!* This well-written, comprehensive, advice-filled book is a welcome tool for all of us—for today and tomorrow."

—Roger E. Herman, *Impending Crisis:*
Too Many Jobs, Too Few People

"*Get a Grip!* is like a user's manual for people living in today's pressure cooker world. Get it today and start to live again!"

—Joe Calloway, *Becoming a Category*
of One

"For those dealing with stress, this is a must-read book. Whether your stress is created from pressures at work or demands at home, Bob Losyk provides a step-by-step process for addressing the physical, mental, and emotional symptoms brought on by a stress-filled life."

—Bill Hardman, President and CEO,
Southeast Tourism Society

"Thankfully, *Get a Grip!* is not overwhelming high tech but is filled with warm, clear, simple, practical ideas. Some books on stress leave me feeling even more uptight because I am not doing things 'right'; however, Bob Losyk's book relaxed me just reading it! Thank you, Bob, for a concise and gentle guide to making our lives even more joyful."

—Barbara Glanz, *Handle with CARE—*
Motivating and Retaining Employees

"If you've ever felt stress slowing down your journey to success (and I assume that includes everyone), this book could change your life. In *Get a Grip!*, Bob Losyk teaches you how stress works, why you feel burned out, and how to put joy back in your life."

—Roger Dawson, *Secrets of
Power Negotiating*

"Feeling overworked, underpaid, overstressed, or burned out? Then get a grip and purchase this book by Bob Losyk. *Get a Grip!* offers practical advice for everyone who is feeling overwhelmed by today's frantic work pace. This is the one thing you must add to your to-do list!"

—Cathy Fyock, *Get the Best*

"Everyone should take the time to read *Get a Grip!* It is a great tool for dealing with stress in today's hectic world. I will share *Get a Grip!* with my co-workers, family, and friends."

—Dean H. Crawford, Senior Vice President,
Yogi Bear's Jellystone Park Camp Resorts

"Stress is a major problem in today's work environment. As a leading expert, Bob Losyk understands how to overcome stress. *Get a Grip!* is a powerful, practical, and informative book for anyone who has a job."

—Marc Slutsky, *Streetfighter Marketing*

"Are you *burned* out? Well, take some *time* out—to read this book. It will show you a *way* out. You'll be glad you did."

—Gregory J.P. Godek, *1001 Ways to
Be Romantic*

"In an age when stress can literally kill, this book is a lifesaver. Bob Losyk truly does have the answers."

—Bill Brooks, *The New Science of Selling and Persuasion*

"*Get a Grip!* could not be more timely. Bob Losyk has provided unique and refreshing ideas that tackle the real intangible facet of our everyday world—stress."

—M. Lance Miller, J.D., Executive Vice President, Metal Treating Institute

"Bob Losyk's *Get a Grip!* is packed with great ideas for those who want to reduce the level of stress in their life."

—Michael LeBoeuf, *How to Win Customers and Keep Them for Life*

"Rarely does a book's title capture the essence of its contents. *Get a Grip!* is sprinkled with practical, real-world scenarios of people with whom we can all relate. Bob Losyk's translation of academic research teaches us lessons about ourselves and others to bring balance and harmony that will clearly resonate with each of us. Enjoy your journey—I know you will."

—Edward E. Scannell, *Games Trainers Play* series

GET A GRIP!

GET A GRIP!

Overcoming Stress and Thriving in the Workplace

BOB LOSYK

WILEY

John Wiley & Sons, Inc.

Published by John Wiley & Sons, Inc., Hoboken, New Jersey.
Published simultaneously in Canada.

For general information on our other products and services, or technical support, please contact our Customer Care Department within the United States at 800-762-2974, outside the United States at 317-572-3993 or fax 317-572-4002.

Wiley also publishes its books in a variety of electronic formats. Some content that appears in print may not be available in electronic books. For more information about Wiley products, visit our web site at www.wiley.com.

Get a Grip! is a trademark belonging to Bob Losyk.

Library of Congress Cataloging-in-Publication Data:

Losyk, Bob.
  Get a grip! : overcoming stress and thriving in the workplace / Bob Losyk.
       p. cm.
  Includes bibliographical references.
  ISBN 0-471-65949-5 (pbk.)
    1. Job stress.   2. Stress management.   I. Title.
  HF5548.85.L67   2004
  158.7'2—dc22
  2004015430

Printed in the United States of America.

10 9 8 7 6 5 4 3 2 1

To the one true love of my life, Lois.

*To my maternal grandparents, Antonio and
Filomena DeAngelo, for their love and inspiration.*

ACKNOWLEDGMENTS

More than anyone else, I must thank my wife, Lois, for her undying love and inspiration, and her steadfast encouragement. Her countless hours of research, suggestions, and insights made this project much easier.

Over the years I have been inspired and informed by many different early researchers, authors, and masters of stress reduction techniques. Some of the authors, such as Hans Selye and Walter Cannon, are mentioned in this book and in the reference section. There are many others, more than I can mention here. I thank all of them for their work. Additionally, I would like to thank all those people who took the time to answer my questions and offer their suggestions and insights.

I thank the many clients who have brought me into their organizations for my consulting services to make positive change within their workforce. Thanks to the many meeting planners and association executives who have used my keynotes and seminars to make a difference with their members. A special acknowledgment goes to the many audience participants who have shared their secrets and ideas on how they deal with everyday stress.

A word of special thanks goes to Matt Holt, editor at John Wiley & Sons, and all the other people at Wiley who interfaced with me. Thank you for your faith in the book and your professionalism. Your suggestions and help made this project come to fruition.

There are some people whose names I must mention, as over the years they have served as a source of inspiration, motivation, information, and laughter. First, there are Gary and Alice Allington, who can truly show anyone how to see the beauty and good in life. Next are Bill Panella and Gerda Carroll, whose sense of humor and fun allow others to realize it is okay to have fun, be silly, and enjoy life to the fullest. Then, there are Donna and Frank Horkey, who have achieved life balance by knowing how to work hard and play hard. Finally, there are my two cousins, both named Ron DeAngelo, who know how to get back up when times are down. I am glad they are all in my life.

Finally, I must mention Beau, my dog, for all the years he has given Lois and me of walking miles and miles, making us laugh, and helping to relax us. His love has deepened our love for each other. He is one of the best destressors we have ever known.

CONTENTS

INTRODUCTION

You must have a lot of stress in your life, otherwise you would not have picked up this book. You are not alone. This is why everyone else takes the book off the shelf. Within the following chapters, you will find help and real solutions. Only you can make the changes. You cannot eliminate all the stressors in your life; no one can. But, you can dramatically reduce them, and have a much better quality of life. You have already taken the first step by picking up and purchasing this book.

Stress may be the biggest single reason we get sick or die prematurely. Every health problem from headaches to heart attacks, from psychosomatic disorders to stroke, can be linked to what is becoming known as the plague of the twenty-first century. Stress quietly builds up in our bodies at work every day, and then we take it home with us, where circumstances so often compound it. We begin the next day starting the cycle all over again, so it continues to build up. Our bodies, minds, and spirits can only take so much. If you ignore the buildup, stress will eventually take its toll.

We must get a grip on stress or pay the price physically, mentally, and spiritually. You cannot rid yourself of all the stress you encounter each day, but you can keep it at a level that has less of a negative impact on your health. If you perform the physical, mental, and spiritual exercises in this book, you will create a positive impact on your health and immensely improve your life. You will improve your thinking and attitude, plus put more fun in your life. There is no downside to destressing.

WHY THIS BOOK?

There are many books available on the subject of stress because it is a common problem. But many of the books are not written for everyone. Some are totally research-based, loaded with research, medical jargon, and footnotes that make it difficult to understand. Other books are written in such an impractical manner that they are difficult to read, let alone implement, and they bounce around from subject to subject.

This book is written with you in mind, whether you are in top or middle management, on the front line, or do not work. *Get a Grip!* is a practical book filled with strategies that work. I realize you do not have hours of free time to implement many complicated, difficult, and time-consuming ideas. That is why I have given you tips and tools that are so easy to use you can practice many of them immediately. The fill-in exercises and most of the ideas and techniques take only a few minutes to do. For those who want to delve further into Eastern practices of meditation and movement, I have given you an introduction to help educate you in order make the decision.

MY APPROACH

I have written this book as if we were having a discussion, or as if you were sitting in one of my stress management seminars. I take a holistic approach, using techniques that integrate the body, mind, and spirit. I give you practical and proven advice and strategies to destress, relax, and recharge. The book provides you with many different techniques to combat and reverse the stress in your life. By having many choices you can pick the methods that you enjoy the most, that fit into your lifestyle, and that mesh with your busy schedule. I realize that not all the methods will appeal to you. Start out slowly with simple practices and work your way up. You cannot master everything instantly. Remember: All journeys begin with the first step.

HOW THE CHAPTERS ARE ORGANIZED

In Chapter 1, I look at why everybody these days is stressed more than ever. I discuss the causes of workplace stress, and the impact it has on organizations. I follow with a discussion in everyday language of what stress is, and the toll it takes on your body, mind, and spirit. You will learn why you must get a grip on stress.

Chapter 2 defines *burnout* and its impact on your health. I take you through the stages of burnout, and help you determine if you are on the path to burnout. You will learn the dangers of becoming burned out, what the warning signs are, and what you can do about it.

In Chapter 3, I show how exercise is the perfect antidote for getting rid of stress. You will learn common sense tips for exercising without having to spend hours of time and money. I will take you through the benefits of strength training, walking, cardiovascular fitness, and other exercises. You can then decide which forms of exercise best fit your lifestyle and schedule.

Meditation is the main theme of Chapter 4. I give you

the many benefits of practicing meditation, as well as the how, when, and where of its practice. I also show you how to use affirmations and visualization. You will learn how to breathe properly to decrease stress, plus simple, yet effective meditations that can be done anytime and in almost any place.

Chapter 5 gives you five more ways to destress. I take you through the basics of stretching and its benefits. You will learn about the healthy benefits of Pilates-based exercise and Yoga. Eastern practices of Tai Chi and ChiGong are explored in enough detail for you to make a decision whether to pursue them further. I debunk some of the false misconceptions about these practices, and show you what wonderful tools they can be for living a more relaxed and happier life.

In Chapter 6 you will discover the role that diet plays in your stress levels. I will tell you how your choices in food can either calm you or stress you. We will look at the real reasons people eat, and how eating healthy can change your mood, your weight, and your physical and mental well-being.

You will learn how lightening up and laughing are powerful stress fighters in Chapter 7. You will discover ways to seek out and find humor where you least expect it. I will show you the benefits of implementing more fun activities in the workplace. I also give you guidelines to make your workplace more fun, creative, and productive.

Chapter 8 helps you to take an up-close look at how you are living your life, what your true priorities are, and shows you how to balance it all. You will realize the dangers of becoming a "slaveaholic," always working more because you are wanting more. You will learn how to leave work behind and to pay more attention to the people and things that really matter to you.

Getting a grip on your time will enable you to feel less stress. In Chapter 9, you will learn to use a time log and find out where your time goes each day. You will find ways to plan and prioritize your day to get more done. Important ways to get rid of interruptions and be more productive are given to you. Finally, you will learn how to clean up your office and home so that they are not bogging you down and stressing you out.

Chapter 10 gives you 50 more ways to lessen the stress in your life. Chapter 11 shows you how to make changes by setting goals. You will create your own action plan so you can implement the changes you need in order to have a more stress-free life.

HOW TO GET THE MOST FROM THIS BOOK

The chapters are arranged in a logical, progressive order. They are also designed so that you can read them in sequence or go to any chapter that catches your interest. I would suggest reading Chapter 1 first so you get an idea of what stress is and what it does to your body. Each chapter is separated into headings and subheadings, so you can quickly find the gist of a topic. You can finish a section, put the book down, and easily come back to the next section.

Do every exercise you can, and keep track of every change you make. It will help you to stay motivated, and enable you to track your progress. This will also help you to be aware of what you have done in the past, and the progress of your changing along the way. Tracking your changes will help you to be more focused, aware, and in control of your stress.

Change is difficult to make. It makes us feel uncomfortable, because our everyday routine is upset. But think about what stress is doing to you, your lifestyle, and the lives of those most near and dear to you. Is this the way you want to live your life? You can go on trapped everyday in a stress-filled world, on your way to burnout and bad health, or you can make the commitment to do something about it. The choice is yours. The solutions are in this book.

GET A GRIP!

1

WHY ARE WE
SO STRESSED OUT?

Work in the twenty-first century is like raising a baby who demands everything at this very moment. Technology cries out at us through computers, cell phones, PDAs, and other gadgets designed to make our lives easier. Our workdays have expanded into our personal lives and it seems the more productive we are, the more the work increases. We can no longer leave work at the workplace. Customers, bosses, and co-workers can contact us anywhere: at home or even in the middle of the night. The dividing line between the workplace and our personal lives has become nonexistent.

Rampant downsizing and layoffs have forced employees to take on the work of those who have left. Organizations of all types are being pushed to do more with less staff. Globalization has added pressure to "go lean." The jobs that were lost in the last recession may never be regained because manufacturing and service jobs are being outsourced and filled with overseas workers.

When you add all of these changes to the demanding pressures of dual-career families, rising healthcare costs, the fear of terrorism, and problems in the Middle East, many people are at the breaking point. They are filled with fear, exhaustion, and anger. More and more people need psychological help and some explode into violence. The term *going postal* has become a common term to express rage. In order to cope, many people engage in unhealthy behaviors such as overeating, smoking, drinking alcohol, and using drugs.

The Marlin Company, a North Haven, Connecticut, workplace communications firm, conducts a survey each year with Harris Interactive entitled "Attitudes in the American Workplace." In their ninth annual survey, they found the following:

- Forty-three percent of American workers say people in their workplace express fear or anxiety about national events at least several times per week.
- Thirty-three percent say they have observed an increase in anxiety or stress-related physical ailments in their workplace (e.g., headaches and colds).
- Twenty-seven percent report an increase in emotional problems such as depression, insomnia, substance abuse, or family conflicts.
- Twenty-eight percent said the economy caused them the most stress.
- Forty-two percent reported an increase in complaints among co-workers in the last year.
- Twenty-seven percent said morale is lower than it was one year ago.
- Thirty-five percent reported an increase in the number of stressed customers.
- Thirty-one percent said there's been an increase in the number of customers who are hard to deal with (Marlin, 2003).

Stress impacts everyone in the workplace. It does not matter what kind of work you do, or what kind of environment from which you come. Whether rich or poor, young or old, male or female, no one is immune from it. Workplace stress greatly impacts our health and well-being as well as the quality of our home life.

The World Health Organization says stress is not just in the United States, but it is a worldwide epidemic. A United Nations report labeled job stress as "the twentieth-century disease." The American Institute of Stress states that stress-related illness costs our economy more than $100 billion per year. The losses in worker productivity hover around $17 billion annually. Stress-related illness and injuries account for almost three-fourths of employee absenteeism. Data from the Bureau of Labor Statistics indicates that workers who take time off for stress-related disorders will be out for about 20 days. The Bureau of National Affairs estimates that 40 percent of all job turnover is due to stress. The estimates are that a mind-boggling 60 to 90 percent of all doctor visits are stress-related (Perkins, 1994). Stress in the workplace along with the stress at home creates a double stress cocktail that has dramatic impact on our lives. In order to live a healthy, prolonged life we have to get a grip on stress.

HOW STRESS IMPACTS THE WORKPLACE

Job-related stress may be the single most important issue affecting the American workplace today. Job stress, simply defined, is when employees cannot meet the demands or requirements of the job. There is too much to do, not enough time, and not enough people or resources to get the job done. In a recent survey of 1,400 people posted online by CareerBuilder.com, more than one-third of respondents stated they experienced an increase in their workload. They claim they are working longer hours and taking shorter lunch breaks to get the job done. As a result, employees start to experience burnout. They simply cannot cope. They begin experiencing many physical and mental symptoms of stress. Not only does the stress take its toll on the workforce, but it also detracts from the overall health of any organization, whether it be profit or nonprofit, educational, or government.

The American Institute of Stress estimated in 2001 that stress cost organizations $300 billion in healthcare, workers compensation, absenteeism, and turnover. Healthcare costs are nearly 50 percent higher for workers who are highly stressed on the job (Goetzel et al., 1998).

The true price tag of stress is much greater than healthcare costs alone. Stress is implicated as a causal factor in: absenteeism, injuries, psychological problems, workers compensation claims, lower productivity, employee theft, low morale, poor performance, and turnover. Obviously, it has a direct impact on the bottom line. The high stress levels that are created in the workplace are not left there. They are brought home to have a negative impact on family life.

Northwestern National Life Insurance, now named ReliaStar Financial Corporation, has conducted several important studies on the impact of stress in the workplace (Northwestern National Life Insurance, 1993). Their conclusions detailed the following statistics:

- One million absences in the workplace were stress related.
- Twenty-seven percent said their job gave them the most stress in their lives.
- Forty-six percent considered the amount of job stress levels as very high or extremely high.
- One-third of workers thought about quitting strictly due to job stress.
- Seventy percent said job stress had impaired their physical and mental health.

WHY THE WORKPLACE IS STRESSING YOU OUT

There are many causes for soaring workplace stress. As you read through the following, think of which ones stress you the most, and how you handle them. If you are in a management position, determine which ones you can change or improve to alleviate the stress levels in your employees.

Physical Conditions

The physical workplace has a great impact on stress levels. Temperature, light, noise, air quality, crowding, isolation, safety, and ergonomic quality all contribute to how a person handles their day. Working in a tiny, impersonal cubicle, in an uncomfortable seat only adds to the stress of the job. Being exposed to difficult surroundings day after day takes a traumatic toll on a person's overall energy, motivation, and health.

Job Design

If it seems we are all doing more work than ever before, it is because we are. Many employees who were downsized or laid off are not being replaced. Yet, most job descriptions are not designed to absorb another whole job. Overwhelming workloads and demands are being placed on workers who remain, and many employees cannot cope.

Most jobs are not designed with the employee's stress levels in mind. Expectations are too high and unrealistic, with too much responsibility placed on one person. The job description includes too many chores and responsibilities, with the additional caveat that it can be updated at any time to include even more tasks. The demands are overwhelming. People are often expected to work long hours with little or no break, doing repetitive tasks. They frequently have no autonomy in doing the job the way they see fit. They often do not have the prerequisite training to do the job right. Eventually, employees start to lose job satisfaction.

Work Roles

When a job is not designed properly, or too many new responsibilities are added to the design, the employees' roles becomes perplexing. Their full role is not clearly spelled out. Employees are not sure of their total responsibilities. Their role becomes conflicted between what they think is expected, and what the boss actually expects. Their role may conflict with or duplicate the role of others, causing clashes between co-workers.

When employees are not sure what the priorities of their role are, they either do what they think is best, or work in a state of confusion. Under constant pressure, they fear that they are doing the wrong task, or doing the right task in the wrong way. Time and energy are sapped creating daily fatigue and frustration.

Technology

Computers, pagers, cell phones, faxes, and the Internet have increased our speed and productivity. People are expected to be more efficient and productive. But, along with new technology comes new stressors. People must constantly be learning new technology and software.

Sometimes the training is inadequate. Sometimes the technology is inadequate. When technology is not working properly, or equipment breaks down, many employees cannot get the work done, and they feel stress begin to rear its ugly head.

Toxic Management

Management style is one of the greatest contributors to stress in the workplace. The old autocratic ruler, a dinosaur of yesteryear, who relentlessly drives their employees, only serves to create stress, burnout, and turnover. Most research indicates that the number one reason for turnover is the management style of the person who is the immediate supervisor. A direct indication of this is the stress that a toxic boss needlessly creates.

Employees are looking for a leader who cares about them. They are looking for someone who asks and respects their opinions, keeps the channels of communication open in all directions, gives quality feedback, recognizes them, and enables them to feel valued.

Relationships with Co-workers

Another major reason for stress is the relationship people have with co-workers. I have had people in companies I consult with tell me that they will stay at their firm because their peers are so terrific. These people really like their co-workers. They can depend on them for help, and can go to them when they need a favor. A real camaraderie and team spirit exists among them.

Unfortunately, this contrasts greatly with the many horror stories I hear of personality clashes and lack of support. Many people think of only themselves and want to protect their own turf. The last few years in many organizations, situations have escalated further into downright rudeness, yelling, and verbal abuse. Many people complain of harassment, threats, intimidation, and actual bullying. The stress that comes from working under these conditions can only be dealt with for so long before it takes an emotional and physical toll. Eventually people burn out or leave.

Time Pressures

People are constantly facing deadlines on tasks, reports, and projects. There is too much work and too little time to do it. It is a continual race against time trying to meet unreasonable deadlines. Some people never get the important tasks accomplished because they are too busy doing what is urgent and putting out fires. Their boss reprimands them for not getting the work done.

As a result, they live from crisis to crisis. This impairs their ability to think clearly and make the right decisions, thus making more mistakes and becoming accident prone. Some people become like pressure cookers, ready to explode. A sign of our times are the new terms *desk rage* and *phone rage.* At the end of the day, many workers are a physical and mental wreck. Symptoms of working under time pressure are: tight stomach and neck muscles, indigestion, pounding heart, nervousness, weakness, anxiety, anger, hostility, insomnia, headaches, and exhaustion.

Job Insecurity

Constant seismic changes in the workplace have created constant stress and insecurity for a lot of employees. Mergers, acquisitions, downsizing, and job outsourcing have made almost unthinkable demands on workers. With so many jobs disappearing over the last few years, a major stressor that impacts employees now is the fear of losing their job. In my seminars, I often ask people what their number one job concern is. Job security always ranks within the top three worries.

A Ladder with No Steps

Those that are secure in their jobs are often concerned that there is no opportunity for training and development. They have no career ladder or path. There are no chances for promotions. When their job becomes a dead end, people become dissatisfied because they cannot fulfill their aspirations. The quality of their work begins to erode; they become frustrated and stressed. Sometimes they withdraw from their co-workers. They eventually begin to look for another job to fulfill their dreams and ambitions.

WHAT IS STRESS?

The term *stress* has been used since the early 1900s to define situations that cause a physiological and psychological change in us. It is difficult to define because it appears in so many forms. Everyone perceives stress differently. Stress can be either harmful or helpful, depending on the circumstances involved. Some stress is beneficial, because it motivates us to improve performance and make changes in our lives. If we had no stress it would prevent us from functioning at all.

In my seminars, I often ask participants to define the term *stress*, and tell me their number one stressor at work. The definitions are all very unique and different. Rarely do two participants mention the same stressor as being the one that impacts them the most. Everyone perceives and reacts to a different stressor in a distinct manner.

No matter which definition we use, it seems that all stress can be separated into two categories: a stimulus or a response (Matteson & Ivancevich, 1987). Stress can be a stimulus, such as a situation or event that happens to us.

The event can be physical or emotional, such as a car accident, an argument at work, the loss of a job, or the loss of a loved one.

Stress can also be the physiological and psychological response we have to that event. It can even be a response to a perceived or unrealistic threat that we worry may happen, such as not getting a promotion at work. In some cases, perception has more influence on us than reality. It does not matter that the event will never happen; just the threat of it is enough to create a stress response.

Stress can come from the demands that we put on ourselves internally, such as trying to be a perfectionist or being liked by everyone. Nothing we do is good enough so we constantly repeat or revise certain tasks to get it exact. Some people spend their entire lives trying to please everyone or win them over. They put tremendous pressure and demands on themselves to achieve an impossible level of perfection and acceptance.

Stress can also be a response to a positive situation, such as moving to a new house, getting a promotion, or a child's upcoming wedding. In some cases, people exhibit fear and anxiety, and some can barely cope. Stress puts an extra demand on bodies, both physically and mentally. I use the term *stressor* to define the situations and events that create a response, and the term *stress* as the body's reaction to that stressor.

The Stress Response

Two people can react differently to the same stressor. What may cause stress to one person can cause excitement and be challenging to another. Some would think nothing of jumping out of an airplane with a parachute and free-falling thousands of feet, while others cringe at the thought. People's personalities and coping styles determine how they will react. This reaction is also influenced by genetic factors, upbringing, lifestyle, overall physical condition, and the stressors and conditions experienced every day.

All the research that has been done on the body's response to stress indicates the same conclusion: The overall human response to stress seems to be universal. The stressors may be different and the stress levels and consequences may vary in individuals, but the response is generally the same when the stressor has a negative impact. Walter Cannon, a Harvard medical doctor, first described the biological response to stress in the 1920s as the *fight-or-flight response* (Cannon, 1929).

When cave people came in contact with dangers like wild beasts, fire, or floods, they had two choices: fight or flee. Their body's biochemistry changed to help them cope with the choice they made. This was an excellent adaptation for survival.

During this fight-or-flight response, the adrenal glands pump adrenaline into the bloodstream to prepare the body for the threat. Other hormones, such as corticosteroids are also released into the bloodstream to mobilize the body and increase energy levels. The heart speeds up and increases the blood supply and flow of oxygen to our muscles. Our blood pressure surges. Our breathing rate snowballs, but each breath may actually be shallower. Our digestive rate diminishes to slow food absorption, so the body can divert the needed sugars and fats to the muscles for energy. We increase our muscular strength as the body prepares to spring into action. Our perspiration increases in order to keep our core body temperature within its normal range.

This physical response has been genetically passed down to us over the centuries and has helped us survive. Although the same biochemical response is still with us, it is not as useful today. It does not fit in our lives. It is ineffective in dealing with our everyday situations, challenges, and hassles. Of course, there are times when we would like to run away or fight back, but unless we are in a life-threatening situation, it would not be appropriate or acceptable. But, our body is still preparing itself for a state of physical readiness just at it did with our early ancestors thousands of years ago.

Reflect for a moment on the number of stressors the cave people had compared to the number of stressors we experience during these frenzied and turbulent times. We are more frequently stressed for longer periods of time than ever before. Plus, many stressors that impact us today are more emotional and psychological, rather than physical. But, our body has a limit on how much stress it can accept and still function normally. The body and mind cannot accept chronic stress over long periods of time and remain healthy. If we do not do something with that stress, the result can lead to sickness, chronic disease, and death. That is why we must get a grip on stress.

The General Adaptation Syndrome

Dr. Hans Selye, an endocrinologist, is known as the founder of stress research and education. Selye spent his career at McGill University, in Montreal, studying and writing about stress from the 1930s to the late 1970s. He left us with hundreds of research articles and over 30 books on the topic. Selye's research indicated that the body goes through a specific patterned response to this extra demand placed on it. He labeled it the *general adaptation syndrome* or GAS (Selye, 1976).

According to Selye, this physical and mental response has three specific stages: alarm reaction, resistance, and exhaustion. In the alarm reaction stage, the body is exposed to the stressor. People become confused and disoriented. The body prepares itself to fight off the stress by sending powerful hormones into the bloodstream. This results in an elevated heart rate and breathing, plus increased muscle tension as the body prepares to spring into action. This defensive move helps us survive the stressor.

In the resistance stage, the hormones in the blood stay at a high level. The body adapts itself to fight off the stress. This adaptation may be in just an isolated organ or a whole organ system. If a high-stress level is continuous, this often can lead to disease in an organ or system. This high level can cause people to also become nervous, fatigued, and often angry.

The final stage is one of exhaustion, where if the stress is ongoing, the organ tissues and the systems may break down. Over a prolonged period this can lead to illness or death. Selye concluded that each person only has a certain amount of adaptation energy to expend on stress. Once this is depleted, we must find a way to replenish the energy, or exhaustion and death set in (Selye, 1976).

The more frequently we are in the fight-or-flight response and go through the three stages, the more wear and tear stress puts on our bodies. The more often the body mobilizes itself for action and depletes its adaptation energy, the greater the toll it takes. At some point, the body can no longer function in a normal manner. If we do not find a way to replenish the energy, the exhaustion reaps havoc on the mind and body, and we become more susceptible to weakness, debility, aging, and eventually death. It is critical that we find a way to restore ourselves back to our normal energy level each and every day. We must get back to a state of balance and equilibrium.

WHAT STRESS IS DOING TO YOU

In order to get a grip on stress, it is important to understand the consequences of negative stressors and the way we react to them. Stress has been implicated as a causal factor in heart disease, stroke, cancer, respiratory disease, arthritis, gastrointestinal disorders, insomnia, psychological disorders (depression, suicide), psychosomatic illness, skin disorders, chronic aches, and pain. (See Figure 1.1.) It is not my purpose to link the onset of all these diseases with stress, or to state that stress is the sole cause of their existence. I strongly feel it is useful to give a brief description of some of the diseases and the significant role that links stress to them. It may motivate you to work to eliminate some of the stress in your life through the methods discussed later.

The Circulatory System

Heart disease is the leading cause of death in the United States. According to the American Heart Association, just under 13 million Americans have coronary artery disease. About a half million people die from heart attacks every year. There is a dramatic amount of evidence showing that our psychological state has a significant impact on heart disease. When people are filled with worry, fear, and rage, they are more prone to heart disease. Since the workplace often

FIGURE 1.1   Impact of Stress

Mental and Emotional Symptoms	Physical Symptoms
Negative attitude	Muscle tightness/soreness
Worry	Muscle spasm
Obsessive thoughts	Headaches
Fear/phobias	Migraines
Sadness	Tight jaw
Irritability	Teeth grinding
Anger/rage	Fatigue/exhaustion
Constant forgetfulness	Constipation
Loneliness	Diarrhea
Confusion	Indigestion
Lack of concentration	Ulcers
Indecisiveness	Trembling
Hopelessness	Asthma
Insomnia	Heart palpitations
Nightmares	High blood pressure
Depression	Shallow, rapid breathing
Suicide	Accident prone

creates these emotions, unless we deal with stress, the chances of developing heart disease increase.

As our heart beats its normal rhythms, transporting our blood, it exerts pressure on the walls of our blood vessels. Our brain works with the heart to keep the rate and blood pressure as low as possible. When we anticipate a negative situation (fear, worry, anxiety), or actually encounter a negative stressor, hormones speed up our heart rate, and our blood pressure is automatically elevated. The heart rushes more blood to vital organs in preparation for fight or flight. We do not realize our blood pressure is rising, because we cannot feel it. In most experiences, the blood pressure returns to its normal range. The dilemma arises when we are constantly raising our blood pressure, due to stress over prolonged periods of time. When the blood pressure continues to stay elevated, it creates a condition known as hypertension. The heart has to work harder to circulate the blood, which increases our risk for heart attack or stroke.

One recent Swiss study by Dr. Georg Noll and his associates showed a clear link between stress and hardening of the arteries, which precedes a heart attack. When patients were subjected to stress tests, their blood vessels would undergo constriction, impeding the blood flow, raising the blood pressure and heart rate (Noll et al., 2002).

The circulatory system transports all the energy to the cells that they need to live, grow, and multiply. In turn, it picks up all the wastes from the cells for elimination. This movement is critical to your survival and as such should not be blocked. Stress forces our brain to send messages to the endocrine and cardiovascular systems, directing the heart and blood vessels to increase their activity. The extra stress-related hormones released into the blood stay there, circulating throughout the body. Fats that are being sent to the muscles for extra energy circulate throughout our blood vessels and can lodge inside them and build up plaque. Over time this leads to narrowing of the blood vessels, blockage, and a condition known as arteriosclerosis. If this blockage is in a coronary artery, it results in a heart attack. The blockage can also occur in other organs such as the brain and kidneys. The risk is always greater when blood pressure is higher.

Stroke

According to the American Heart Association, every minute a person in the United States suffers a stroke. The only diseases that cause more deaths are heart attacks and cancer. The most common type of stroke is a blockage of a blood vessel in the brain. This occurs when a piece of plaque breaks off the inside of a blood vessel somewhere in the body and is transported to the brain. This blockage disrupts the needed flow of blood to the brain.

Researchers at the University of Michigan, along with doctors in Finland, studied 2,300 men in Finland. The researchers subjected the men to various stressors, measured their blood pressure before and after, and monitored them for 11 years. The men whose blood pressure rose from the stressors had a staggering 72 percent greater chance of developing a stroke than those whose blood pressure was lower from the same stress (Everson et al., 2001). The message is clear: Stress is linked to increased blood pressure, heart attack, and stroke.

Muscles and Bones

Because of the fight-or-flight syndrome, stress makes our muscles tense as the body gets ready to spring into action. The body responds this way whether the threat is real or perceived. Muscles that are chronically tensed will contract and become shortened. When this happens, they pull on ligaments, tendons, and joints, creating pain. Muscles also become weak and fatigued, creating headaches (including migraines), backaches, and pain in various areas of the body such as the neck, shoulder blades, and knees.

The Gastrointestinal System

Stress is brutal on the gastrointestinal (GI) system. When we are under great stress, the salivary glands can stop the flow of saliva, or in other cases, make too much. The stomach increases its secretions of acids creating excess acid, nausea, and ulcers. Another result of stress, and maybe the most common, is diarrhea. Many people also complain about the muscle tightening that takes place in the stomach area.

The Immune System

The immune system functions as a defense that detects invading microbes and destroys them. When the system is under stress, our immunity becomes compromised, and we are more susceptible to colds, the flu, and other types of infection. Julie Kiecolt-Glaser and Ronald Glaser reviewed a number of studies that demonstrated the link between stress and the immune system. Many people in the studies were under severely stressful events such as sleep deprivation and being recently widowed. Some were under less severe stress for a shorter duration. All showed evidence of a decrease in the specific cells that fight disease, such as T-cells and other antibodies (Kiecolt-Glaser & Glaser, 1993).

In another widely reported experiment, first published in the *New England Journal of Medicine*, a link was established between stress and the common cold. Subjects under stress were exposed to the common cold virus by use of a nasal spray. Another group, not under stress, was exposed to the same virus. The group under stress was more than twice as likely to contract the cold. Apparently, people not under stress have a greater ability to fight off cold germs than those who are under stress (Cohen, Tyrell, & Smith, 1991).

Asthma

When we breathe under normal resting conditions, our breathing fits a regulated pattern. The muscles in the chest are relaxed, and the lungs allow the air to flow in and out freely as the diaphragm rises up and down. Bronchial tubes divide into small balloonlike sacs, or alveoli that circulate air throughout the lungs.

Asthma is most often precipitated by specific allergens. However, asthma can also be caused by nonallergic triggers such as stress, fear, fatigue, and anxiety. There are many cases of highly stressful situations precipitating an asthma attack. Such events as a death in the family, a car accident, or even a visit to the dentist can set off a severe asthma attack.

In a typical attack, the chest muscles begin to tighten, breathing becomes faster, and at the same time, shallower. Cases of extreme stress may tighten the bronchial tubes. The alveoli constrict, cutting down the regular flow of oxygen. The linings of the bronchial tubes swell and become inflamed. They may fill with thick mucus, creating a wheezing sound. These changes make breathing difficult. Each breath takes in less air, putting stress on the entire body.

Cancer

Stress by itself does not cause cancer. Many factors determine the link between stress and cancer. However, under certain conditions, stress can lower the ability of our immune system to fight off the growth of abnormal cells. Much research is now being conducted to determine the conditions of how and when stress lowers our immunity.

Cancer occurs when normal cells in our body change into abnormal or malignant cells. They grow in an uncontrolled fashion and take over the normal cells. With enough white blood cells, we can usually fight off this abnormal growth. When people are constantly exposed to severe stress, certain hormones decrease in our bloodstream. This causes the white blood cells to begin to diminish in number, preventing them from destroying the cancer cells. This greatly increases the possibility that the cancerous cells will continue to grow and create a tumor.

Depression

It is not clear whether depression is caused solely by stress, as some depression seems to also be related to a chemical imbalance and can be hereditary in nature. But, it cannot be disputed that depression seems to be a frequent symptom of stress. Depression is characterized by a chronic sense of feeling down or sad. The body feels weak, nervous, and the mind is unable to concentrate. There is a total lack of energy and interest in doing anything. Depressed people want to stay in bed and sleep. Depression is often related to certain events at work such as lost sales, lost promotion, constant conflict with other people, and constant changes in the work environment.

Psychosomatic Illness

Psychosomatic illness is one in which the body is directly influenced by the negative thought processes of the mind.

A person's negative state of mind lessens their ability to ward off disease, and enables it to gain a foothold in the body. As you react to everyday stressors, what you tell yourself has a great impact on your body's reaction. It is not so much what happens to you, as it is how you react with your mind, and what you do about it. The subject of the mind-body connection will be discussed in greater detail in Chapter 4.

2

GET A GRIP OR BURN OUT

Although not a new phenomenon, job burnout has become a modern day by-product of continuous job stress. "Burnout is a psychological process, brought about by unrelieved work stress, that results in emotional exhaustion, depersonalization, and feelings of decreased accomplishment" (Matteson & Ivancevich, 1987). Job burnout is accompanied by a feeling of mental and physical fatigue either before, during, or after the workday. It most commonly impacts people who work long hours, in highly stressful jobs, in which they have made a very special commitment.

BURNOUT'S IMPACT

Many situations and events in the workplace may contribute to burnout. (See Figure 2.1.) The following are true stories of everyday, real people, impacted by job burnout.

Tom

Tom is a junior high school math teacher who had always loved his job. A bright and gifted teacher, he taught the advanced math classes. His classes were the epitome of

FIGURE 2.1   Job Factors That Lead to Burnout

Demanding boss

Time pressure

Overwhelming workload

Unsafe work environment

Job insecurity

Lack of policies and procedures

Rigid policies and procedures

Constantly changing policies and procedures

Decreasing benefits

Role ambiguity or conflict

Lack of training

Lack of communication

Lack of feedback

Lack of support

Lack of recognition

Lack of employee involvement

Little chance for promotion

No career path

Conflict with co-workers

Repetitive tasks and activities

Downsizing

involved, high-learning students, who were wonderfully well behaved. Once, Tom became teacher of the year for the entire county. All the teachers, parents, and students highly respected and loved him. He had a great relationship with his principal.

After 15 years, the principal decided to retire. The new administrator who took over decided to make some changes. She wanted to increase the math scores of the lowest level children. After 17 years of enjoyable and rewarding teaching, Tom was given a new assignment: teach basic math skills to children who really did not want to learn.

Though slightly reluctant, he undertook his job with great enthusiasm. He was not prepared for the challenges ahead. Tom always had students who came to class ready and eager to learn. The first day of this class was a rude awakening. Students immediately began to demonstrate behaviors that Tom had never had to deal with before. They pushed the limits to see what they could get away with. When Tom sent them to the principal for misbehaving, the new principal blamed him for not knowing how to discipline his students.

Within a few weeks, Tom started to feel a sense of tiredness at the end of each day, which would not go away. He developed migraine headaches, which he never had before. He had trouble getting out of bed in the morning and felt nauseous as he drove to work. He stopped taking part in any after-school activities. He argued frequently with his wife and was quite nasty to his three children. Tom was beginning to feel the classic symptoms of job burnout.

Rosa

After working as a paralegal for five years, Rosa felt very confident in her abilities and enjoyed her career. She took great interest in the cases she assisted her attorney with, and even dreamed of someday going back to college and becoming an attorney. She was considering this until the firm she worked for assigned her to an additional attorney with a heavy caseload of complicated cases. Now Rosa was working for two attorneys, and this new attorney was treating her like a slave. Working 12 to 14 hours a day, she had no time for anything else in her life, and being a single mother of a 12-year-old, she virtually had no time to spend with her daughter. She was afraid to complain to the office manager because the firm had high expectations of employee commitment; everyone was expected to do what was needed. Paralegal jobs were hard to come by, and this was a highly prestigious firm. She could easily be replaced.

Rosa was feeling trapped. It seemed that she was constantly sick with a cold, sore throat, or whatever was going around the office. This made it even harder to cope. Every sick day she took put her further behind. She found that she could never get enough sleep and was always feeling exhausted. Mistakes started showing up in her work, and because she was so conscientious, she started to have negative feelings about her abilities. Sometimes Rosa would go into the stall in the women's bathroom and just cry. She was feeling so depressed! Eventually, she found herself in a daze. She couldn't focus on any of the cases. She would just sit in her office and stare at a piece of paper for half an hour at a time.

The day of reckoning came at the monthly staff meeting where everyone had to give a progress report on their cases. Rosa had nothing to report. She had done nothing of any consequence for a month. The afternoon of the staff meeting she fled the office, and could not bring herself to return. Rosa knew she was out of a job.

Brad

Brad was the owner of a small travel agency and was well known and popular within the community. He was highly involved in county chambers and associations, and helped plan many travel-related events. He never made a lot of money from his business, but it was certainly enough for him and his wife to pay their bills and take frequent discounted trips. Brad had three other travel agents working for him. After many good years, events started to change. The airlines decided they were going to change the way they did business with travel agents and deeply cut the commissions they paid to agents for each airline ticket that was written.

Brad had to charge his clients a service fee for each ticket. Many of his clients, especially the corporate ones, refused to do business with him anymore and went directly to the airlines to avoid the fee. This cut his net profits by 40 percent. Brad had to let go of two of his agents. All of a sudden, he was trying to carry the load of the two employees that were gone. He was under severe stress, and started to exhibit many emotional and physical symptoms of burnout. He became exhausted, and starting making mistakes, upsetting many of his long-time clients.

Within a few months, discount travel web sites started popping up. Brad began to lose more business. After 27 years of running his agency, he was faced with the prospect of losing it. When he put out feelers about selling the business, he discovered that its value had greatly diminished. Life as he knew it was coming to an abrupt end. It ripped him apart like nothing before.

Brad took it hard and could not cope with the stress. He began drinking and taking tranquilizers. A once mellow and happy guy became angry, dazed, and confused. He made poor business decisions, and wound up letting someone practically steal the agency out from under him. He and his wife drifted apart as he withdrew and sank into depression. They soon divorced, and Brad moved away from all his friends and family. Brad never recovered and lives lonely and isolated in a trailer camp today, with Social Security being his only means of income.

WHAT IS BURNOUT?

Tom, Rosa, and Brad are some examples of what burned out workers experience: a declining emotional process that leads to a declining energy level. They become habitually fatigued, and their resistance to sickness lessens. People lose their enthusiasm and develop a negative attitude toward work and the people around them. Sometimes they withdraw from any conversation, except only that which is necessary.

Burned out workers develop a debilitating feeling of cynicism, pessimism, and hopelessness. Their goal is to just get through the day. Many people feel they are no longer contributing or accomplishing anything at work. They experience self-doubt. There is a decline in their commitment to getting the job done. As the person withdraws from the workplace, productivity declines, while tardiness and absenteeism increases. People take longer breaks, spend more time at coffee machines and water coolers, and procrastinate with their work. (See Figure 2.1.)

People bring home the physical and mental symptoms of burnout, which have a negative impact on family life. If there is more stress at home, from family demands and conflicts, it has further impact on people's exhaustion level. In a dual-career couple, this creates even greater problems, especially if both partners are burned out. The burned out person begins to withdraw from their family. Burnout eventually reaches the critical stage and the person cannot function. The family may begin to fall apart, which in turn creates even more debilitating stress for everyone.

THE FOUR STAGES OF BURNOUT

Burnout is not something that just happens overnight. It is a long developing process, often with early undetected signs and symptoms. Many researchers (Veninga & Spradley, 1981) have distinguished burnout as five distinct stages. My own research has led me to identify four distinct stages, with the last stage resulting in three choices.

Stage One: Turned On

The first stage occurs consistently when we accept a new job or new position, or become involved in a new project. A high level of enthusiasm, abundant energy, and the desire to be involved and productive characterizes this stage. The job almost becomes the "be all, end all" in our lives. We have a powerful desire to be successful in the new endeavor. Some people are able to cope with the demands and pressures of this stage. They stay turned on for many years. They learn to manage the stress and never enter into the next stage. Yet, others begin to burn up too much adaptation energy, start to fatigue, and exhibit the symptoms of stage two.

Stage Two: Turned Off

The turned off stage sneaks up on us slowly, often existing for a while, yet overlooked. It starts with the job not turning out to be all we thought it would be. As our expectations diminish and disillusionment increases, energy starts to sink and enthusiasm begins to wither. We begin to exhibit daily tiredness, which shifts to chronic fatigue. We start to withdraw from others and avoid work. Feelings of cynicism, sadness, and confusion start to overwhelm us. We have doubts about our abilities and the contributions that we are making at work. Tom, the teacher, is a good example of stage two.

Stage Three: Wiped Out

In the wiped out stage, we have a rude awakening that we are in trouble. Our fatigue turns to exhaustion. Our sadness and confusion turn to depression. We have trouble eating and sleeping. These symptoms, coupled with the lack of energy and negative thinking, lower our resistance and make us more susceptible to disease. We cannot focus, make decisions, or get the job done. We only have a limited amount of adaptation energy. We experience a general feeling of malaise. We start to exhibit pain in the head, neck, back, and shoulders. The stress also impacts our heart and blood pressure. Emotionally and physically, like Rosa the paralegal, we are in a crisis.

Stage Four: Get a Grip or Burn

The last stage I have termed *get a grip or burn*. This stage has been described by Veninga and Spradley as "hitting the wall" (1981). We are in a desperate stage of despair. We are so emotionally wrecked and physically sick that we must make some critical choices. We can either go on as we are—totally burned out, and risk severe chronic disease, such as heart attack and stroke, and/or death—or we can make changes—by switching either jobs or careers. The third choice is to stay in the same job and seek medical help and counseling, and immediately embark on a rigid stress-reduction program. However, it may be too late for the latter choice. Some people can recover over time, but others cannot. Brad, the travel agent, was a perfect example of someone who never did recover. It's imperative that we recognize the problem in stage two and make a change before the stress gets totally out of control. This is when we must decide to begin a stress-reduction program or seek some change that will prevent the burnout.

Not everyone suffers from burnout. The type of organization and position, plus salary and benefits, all play a major role in how stress affects people. The relationships with co-workers and management have a great impact. The emotional and physical well-being of the person also factors into whether burnout will happen. Last, but not least in importance, is what the individual is doing to relieve job stress each day, and recharge body, mind, and spirit for the next day.

Do you think you suffer from job burnout? If not today, could it happen tomorrow? Take the survey in Figure 2.2. Find out if you are on your way to a crisis that could have a great impact on your health, and decide what changes you need to make in your life. Add up your score and read the concluding interpretation.

GETTING A GRIP ON BURNOUT

In my seminars, I ask people to make a commitment to making change. If you do nothing, nothing will change. The old adage, "nothing ventured, nothing gained" truly does apply. I am asking you to employ as many of the following tips as apply to you, in order to prevent yourself from heading down that dangerous road to burnout. It is a road from which it is hard to return.

FIGURE 2.2 Burnout Assessment

Read each statement below. At the right of the statement fill in the number that most accurately reflects how you feel or what you believe. Use the following rating scale:

1 = Never   2 = Seldom   3 = Occasionally   4 = Frequently   5 = Always

You   *Score*

Have trouble getting out of bed in the morning and facing the day.   _____

Feel sad, anxious, or depressed on the way to work.   _____

Have trouble starting working in the morning or after lunch.   _____

Have a lack of energy during the workday.   _____

Find yourself frequently getting sleepy or nodding off during the workday.   _____

Daydream or have trouble focusing on the task at hand.   _____

Attempt to stay isolated from others while at work.   _____

Dread attending meetings.   _____

Suddenly burst into tears.   _____

Feel overwhelmed by the amount of work.   _____

Believe no one cares about you or your work.   _____

Believe your work is boring.   _____

Believe you are underpaid.   _____

Think you are not contributing during the day.   _____

Feel little job satisfaction.   _____

Have trouble meeting deadlines.   _____

Avoid or postpone making important job-related decisions.   _____

Feel exhausted at the end of the workday.   _____

Are a couch potato at home after work.   _____

Have trouble sleeping at night.   _____

Total Score: _____

FIGURE 2.2 *(Continued)*

Interpreting Your Score

85–100: You are highly burned out and filled with great stress. You must undertake a stress-reduction program immediately, both on and off the job, or risk sickness and disease. Consider getting psychological help and also counseling at work. If you have not had a physical exam in the last year, make an appointment with your doctor immediately.

70–84: You are undergoing high to high-moderate levels of stress and rapidly approaching burnout, if you have not already begun the initial stages. Again, a stress-reduction program is suggested, both during the workday and after it. Changes in your work situation should be discussed with your supervisor in order to prevent burnout.

55–69: You may not realize it or feel it, but you still have a good possibility of job burnout. Some form of stress reduction is still indicated to rejuvenate yourself each day and prevent burnout.

40–54: You are not under great stress and are not prone to burnout. Just be aware of the stress levels at the end of each day, and take action if and when needed.

Take a Good Look

You have already taken one step toward dealing with burnout simply by having read about the stages of burnout, and taking the burnout assessment. Now that you understand burnout and how it works, you need to make an honest assessment of your job and workplace. The best way to make change is to first take an honest look at your job situation, and assess why you are becoming burned out. Be truthful with yourself, and do not be in denial. Ask yourself:

- What working conditions are creating the negative emotion and physical state?
- What conditions can I change?
- What situations are impossible to change that I must accept?
- Is it worth accepting, or should I move on?

You need to know the root causes that create this negative psychological state. Then you must decide if staying in the situation is worth the price you are paying, both physically and mentally. If not, then it is time to change.

Stay Up When Times Are Down

Although this will be covered in more detail in the following chapters, it is important to realize the impact of your attitude on whether and when you burn out. Our attitude is the way we view the events of the day, and ultimately how we assess those events. We can view them through either a positive or a negative prism giving positive or negative meanings to the events. Positive thinking creates a positive attitude and belief system. We look for the good in situations, which enables us to stay focused. When focused, we can make positive decisions and take positive action. This can help in delaying burnout or making the right decisions to prevent it.

Negative thinking only creates negative attitudes, beliefs, and feelings. You develop a negative personality. Remember: Your body hears everything your mind tells it. The more negative input that goes into your mind, the more negative reaction your body has. This all contributes to greater stress. With a negative perspective, you not only crash and burn, but you burn out faster and more severely.

Try to monitor your thought process. Hear what you tell yourself and how you react to the day's events. Listen to the negative self-talk. Change it into positive self-talk. It may not ease the sequence of events of the workday, but it will definitely help how you feel at the end of each day. It also aids the way you feel at the beginning of the next day.

Learn to Say No

Talk to your boss about the responsibilities you have, especially if you are overwhelmed and overworked. Some of us cannot learn to say no, so the boss gives us more to do. The added weight keeps dragging us down. Sometimes you must refuse additional demands on your time. If people leave and are not replaced, and you must do their job as well, you might want to let your supervisor know how that will impact you and your health, if you feel they will be open-minded and understanding.

Do Not Be an Isolationist

Do you stay in your cubicle or keep your door closed all day so you can be more productive? Do you eat lunch at your desk instead of with your colleagues? Have you isolated yourself from your co-workers? Do not feel that you always have to go it alone. We need other people for many reasons, but certainly the right people can act as a sounding board. Expressing yourself to others about some things that are up-setting you does not portray you as weak. It shows you are human. It also gives us new insights and ideas.

Hearing other people's concerns and challenges makes us realize we are not alone in our feelings. It gives us a differ-ent, and perhaps new, perspective. Other people can be nur-turing and help us get through the day. Being connected to our co-workers, especially ones with positive attitudes, can help eliminate stress. If you do not trust your co-workers or if it is detrimental politically to confide in them, then talk to friends and family that have your best interest at heart. Build relationships with people who have great attitudes.

Do Not Be a Perfectionist

People who suffer from burnout are often perfectionists. They spend too much time and energy getting the job done exactly right instead of just getting the job done. Perfectionists are also idealistic about the way things should be. The "should be's" can drive you down the path of burnout very quickly. You will constantly be frustrated by the way you think things should be versus the way they are. Stop looking for the faults and flaws in the system or in others. Get a grip on your perspective.

Get Organized

Being disorganized is one of the leading causes of job stress. Clean your desk or work area before you leave each day, and make a to-do list for tomorrow. You can prioritize it in the morning when your mind is clearer. If your desk is sloppy when you come in the next day, it just creates wasted time and energy. You cannot work on 10 different things at once, so why have them in front of you? This only prevents you from concentrating on your priorities. Put things away in files or electronic files. Learn to use technology as a personal information retrieval system to save time and prevent stress.

Make planning and prioritizing a critical part of your day. Always work on those tasks and projects that get results. Perform the activities that are critical to keeping your job. Work on those items that are important, but not yet urgent. That way, you complete the job before it becomes urgent. You do not want to spend all your time operating in a crisis mode putting out fire after fire.

Delegate and Empower Your People

If you are a manager or supervisor, take a good look at what you do each day. Keep a record of your daily activities so you know exactly which tasks are accomplished each day. Ask yourself which ones really annoy you. This raises your awareness of activities that are draining your energy. Then ask yourself which tasks or responsibilities can be delegated. Stop thinking you are the only one who could perform these tasks correctly. You could certainly delegate the ones that are routine and too easy, that others could perform. Give other people the responsibility to do tasks that take a large chunk of your time. Consider delegating projects that you are least qualified to do or ones you absolutely hate to do.

Empower your people to make decisions when you are not there. Empowerment simply means giving them the authority and responsibility to make decisions when management is absent. If your people must come to you and ask you for a decision, then they are not empowered in that area. But, you cannot empower people without training and communication. You must let them know what they can and cannot do. Employees must also feel comfortable that if they make a mistake, they can still come to you for help. Both delegating and empowering are potent tools for freeing up more energy for your workday.

Be Aware of How You Feel

Many people just plow through the day never taking the time to feel what their body is telling them. They are so caught up in work that they ignore the signals the body is sending them. A good way to get in touch with your body is to sit in a chair and let every muscle in your body relax. Then focus on areas where you feel tenderness or pain. Are there any muscles that are tight or tingling? Notice your pulse (the best place is the right side of the neck, just below the jaw). Is it racing? What does your stomach feel like? Is it tied up in knots or feeling nauseous? Your body will let you know if it is out of synch, if you take the time to monitor it.

Take Care of Your Mind and Body

You cannot work an extra-long day under stress and pressure without taking breaks. Do not skip lunch. Try a healthy, low-fat, low-sugar snack twice a day. It gives you something to look forward to during the day. Get away from the desk or work area for breaks and for lunch. Eating and working are bad for your digestive process. You're eating under duress.

Take a few minutes to do some quick stress-reduction exercises (see Chapter 3). If you have a job that keeps you sedentary all day, get up once every hour, move the body, and stretch. Movement and stretching prevents back problems, muscle tightness, and other pain. Consider meditating, which will be discussed in detail in Chapter 4. You only need 5 to 15 minutes to achieve a feeling of relaxation and calm.

After work, find an enjoyable activity that clears your mind, even if it is for just a short time. Find something to do where you are not thinking about work. This could be exercise or a sport, meditation or deep relaxation, or a hobby. The point is that you just cannot come home, eat dinner, and become a couch potato. It does not get rid of the day's stress. Some physical action or mind-cleansing activity will serve to recharge your mind and body for the next day.

If you find that you are having trouble coping with your job mentally, consider discussing it with your boss. If this is not feasible, then set up a meeting with an Employee Assistance Professional, if one is available at your workplace.

Take Time Off

Since companies started downsizing, merging, and reengineering, the sabbatical has virtually disappeared. Unfortunately, with all the people being laid off, and everyone else picking up the slack, sabbaticals are needed more than ever. Sadly, they have been replaced by sick leave. A sabbatical is simply taking off an extended period of time in order to recharge and renew yourself. Sometimes people need a few weeks, others need a few months. A sabbatical is very effective when you have reached the get a grip or burn stage of burnout. Whether you have made the decision to change your position, or job, some time off can really help to restore your depleted stock of adaptation energy. It can greatly enhance your vitality and resilience.

3

Shaping Up to Keep Stress Down

Think back to Chapter 1 where I discussed the fight-or-flight response. The body readies itself to spring into action when there is a real or perceived threat. When activated, hormones produced from this response flow throughout your system and stay in the bloodstream until your body uses them up. Sometimes it can take hours after the threat has gone away. You must rid the body of these substances or else they become dangerous to your health. If not disposed of, over time, your organs can become impaired or diseased.

When you are under tension and stress at work, your muscles contract, but not to the degree they would if you needed to fight someone or run away from a threat, as our primitive ancestors did. Even though the threat is different, your body still prepares for physical activity, and even though the muscle response is much less, your muscles still tense up. Sometimes they can stay that way for hours, and you may not even notice it. If you do not do something about this tension, it eventually causes body aches, pains, spasms, and injuries. Over a long period of time, it tends to become chronic.

This state of lesser tension also leads to elevated blood pressure, faster heartbeat, and rapid, shallower breathing. You may not notice this tension in the beginning, but if it continues over a long period of time, it can lead to other conditions such as permanent high blood pressure, heart problems, gastrointestinal disorders, or urinary problems.

A perfect example of this state of lesser tension is a traveler who is nervous on airplane flights. He may hold on to the armrest or seat so tightly that he is responsible for the term *white knuckle flyer.* Similarly, most people have no problem driving in normal traffic, but when others get on a freeway they get very nervous and grip the steering wheel for dear life. Another example is a salesperson who is trying to close a deal with a client, and she is squeezing a coffee cup, glass, or pen because of muscle tension. She may rub her fingers together or squeeze her own arm or hands without realizing it. Again, none of this stress is life threatening, but it takes its toll over time. Whether it be from anger, worry, or fear, in every case the tension, stress, and pressure must be relieved. The stress hormones must be reduced.

Fortunately, there is a simple answer to solving the body's buildup of unwanted substances: exercise. The American Council on Exercise states that exercise is one of the most effective ways to reduce stress and its effects on the body. Its mental and physical benefits are without rival. I define exercise as anytime we move muscles, bend joints, and move the bones in a repetitive fashion. Exercise can be many different sports and activities with a variety of forms and variations. The important thing is that you are moving the body. Body movement equals less stress, so you have got to get moving. Move it and lose it!

WHY WORKING OUT KEEPS THE STRESS OUT

Your body has already prepared itself for a physical response when stress has triggered it, so you might as well use the body's cue. Exercise helps our bodies get rid of the by-products created by the physical stress response. It actually decreases the stress hormones that are released throughout the workday. Exercise gets our muscles back to a state of normalcy, strengthens and tones them, and helps us respond better to later stressors. The mental benefits are just as great as the physical ones, because exercise helps us to feel peaceful and relaxed. It gives us a sense of calm. For many, it has a tranquilizing effect during which people can reflect on important elements of life such as relationships or spirituality. It also helps people to focus on and solve problems. (See Figure 3.1.)

Exercise has a tremendous benefit on the cardiovascular system. The American Heart Association states that lack of exercise and a sedentary lifestyle are major causes of heart disease. Your heart, being a muscle, needs exercise just like other muscles. A lack of exercise makes your heart weaker.

Speeding up the heart rate during exercise strengthens the heart and makes it work more efficiently while it is resting. The conditioned heart at rest beats slower than the out-of-shape heart. With each beat, the stronger heart pumps more volume of blood than the unconditioned heart. The number of smaller blood vessels that supply the heart (capillaries) actually increase in number, allowing greater blood flow to the heart itself. Exercise also lowers the blood pressure against the vessel walls, thus preventing hardening of the arteries. Dr. Kenneth Cooper, the famed cardiologist, claims that aerobic exercise can also help you survive a heart attack.

FIGURE 3.1 Benefits of Exercise

Exercise has been indicated to provide the following health benefits:

- Reduces fear, worry, anxiety, anger, and mild depression.
- Improves your mood and attitude.
- Increases concentration.
- Improves muscle mass, strength, and tone.
- Strengthens the heart and increases its efficiency.
- Boosts energy levels.
- Improves bone density.
- Reduces high blood pressure.
- Increases immunity to respiratory diseases.
- Lowers cholesterol and triglycerides.
- Reduces the risk of certain cancers.
- Eliminates different types of aches and pains.
- Reduces the chance of diabetes.
- Improves diet; maintains or decreases weight.
- Aids in sleeping.
- Increases self-esteem.

Exercise also improves the ability of your lungs to expand and take in more air. Because of this, your lungs and heart work together in a more efficient manner. As your heart becomes more fit, pumping more blood, that increased amount of blood picks up more oxygen in the capillaries of the lungs and delivers it to the cells throughout the body. As a result, your stamina and endurance increases. You do not get fatigued as quickly during everyday tasks and activities. People that exercise have fewer respiratory diseases such as colds, the flu, and pneumonia.

Exercise increases the amount of endorphins the body produces. Endorphins are chemicals that are produced in the brain that send signals to the nervous system. They act like pain killing medicine. When we undergo prolonged exercise, we increase the flow of these endorphins. In addition to killing pain, endorphins increase our ability to fight disease, reduce our appetite, and give us a sense of euphoria. Endorphins are a natural high.

Why So Many Couch Potatoes?

If it is universal that everyone feels better and less stressed after exercise, then why aren't more people doing it? There are two main reasons (excuses is a better word): time and energy. Many of us go through life each day at a frantic pace, with very little free time. Most people feel they are just too exhausted after work to find the energy. That is why the remote control and hands-free devices are so popular. People just want to melt into a couch and not move. For some, the term *exercise* conjures up visions of strenuous activity, usually at a gym. In reality, it is all about perception. They perceive that they will have to put out more energy doing something that is not fun or enjoyable.

Okay, so you say you do not have any free time to exercise. You can still gain benefits by doing short spurts of exercise. I am not asking you to perform the usual prescribed regimen of one hour, three days a week where it feels more like punishment than anything else. I know human nature is such that you will not commit to changing your entire lifestyle to fit in exercise. We all need something that fits our schedule and is realistic. But, everybody can find three to five minutes here and 10 minutes there. To relieve stress, it is not so much how long you work out, but how much total exercise time you accrue in a day. If it adds up to 30 or 45 minutes, then you have done a good job of destressing.

Okay, so you say you are too exhausted to exercise. Just about everyone can find the energy to exercise for three to five minutes. You will find that exercise is a great remedy for the fatigue that comes with burnout that I discussed in Chapter 2. In actuality, after a few weeks, exercise increases your energy and stamina. You begin to feel you cannot do without it.

Okay, so you say you cannot stand the way your body looks. Seeing the exercise machine infomercials or ads for health clubs and gyms sends the message that exercise is for the young and good looking. It is no wonder we are intimidated by these perfect, hard bodies. How absurd! Exercise benefits anyone of any age. Exercise benefits people into their eighties and nineties. Even if you have not exercised for years, it is not too late to start. You do not need to wear tight fitting, skin bearing workout outfits to exercise. If you are concerned about the way you look, then consider beginning at home.

COMMON SENSE TIPS FOR GETTING STARTED

If you have led years of a sedentary lifestyle, and if you have not exercised in a long time, first consider a physical exam to be sure there are no problems. (See Figure 3.2.) If you have chronic health problems or recent injuries definitely discuss your plans with a physician. If you are a male over 40 or a female over 50 years of age and overweight, you may want to undertake a stress test. Doctors hook you up to an electrocardiogram (EKG) while you walk on a treadmill. I have taken one, and it is nothing more than a walk that gets progressively faster and gets your heart rate up. This is a good test to determine heartbeat irregularities and signs of arteriosclerosis.

If you have always been out of shape, the last thing you want to do is start vigorous exercise or begin running with-

FIGURE 3.2   Health Quiz

Before starting an exercise program, it is a good idea to assess your health. You need to be sure that exercising will not impact you negatively. If you answer yes to any of these statements, please discuss them in detail with your physician, along with your exercise goals, and get his or her approval first.

	Yes	No
I live a sedentary lifestyle and rarely exercise.	___	___
I have a medical history that includes heart problems.	___	___
My immediate family has a history of heart problems.	___	___
I take medicine for high blood pressure.	___	___
I take medication that might interfere with exercise.	___	___
I have high cholesterol.	___	___
I have asthma or trouble breathing.	___	___
I smoke cigarettes, cigars, or pipes.	___	___
I have another medical condition that might prevent me from exercising.	___	___
I am 20 pounds or more overweight.	___	___
I have pain and stiffness in my joints.	___	___
I get weak, exhausted, or dizzy after any physical activity.	___	___

out a medical exam. Your heart is weak from lack of use and could be shocked by sudden exercise into a heart attack. Your heart attack chances are greater if you have high cholesterol and your artery walls are weakened or have become lined with plaque.

Set Objectives and Goals

Many of us believe that we do not have the money, time, or energy for exercise. But, there are many different ways you can exercise. Some are more strenuous than others, and some take more time. Some can be done alone, while some must be performed with others. Some can be done at work. Many are free and require little equipment.

Pick an activity or exercise that you feel is the most fun and practical, and easiest for you. If you think running is not for you, then why bother? If you have physical limitations that prevent you from lifting weights, then do not attempt it. You must decide whether the activity you choose realistically fits your current state of health and lifestyle.

If you need the time alone to recharge, then go solo. However, sometimes working out with family or friends can also enhance your enjoyment and keep you motivated. If you feel you need to join a class to be motivated, and also enjoy the social benefits, then go that route. Ask yourself if you have the money to pay for and use a health club membership or will you let it go to waste? The key is to pick an exercise that you will enjoy and want to continue.

A word of caution is due here. Some people take up a game or sport they like, but they are highly competitive. Pretty soon, it is no longer just a game, but becomes a win at all costs. This does not lead to stress reduction. In fact, quite the opposite happens. If you are a highly competitive person, be aware of this. Even if you decide to go solo, do not try to outdo yourself each time. You get to the point where it is no longer fun, and it creates negative feelings and stress if you do not do more each time.

Set a goal to make time for exercising, either before, during, or after the workday. In other words, write it down on your to-do list. Just like you would not skip a meal, do not skip exercise. Consider giving up something else that is less important, such as watching TV or Web surfing. Think of it as a minivacation. Make it a long-term commitment. Make it a way of life. What is more important than improving your health?

Use It: Do Not Abuse It

Start out slow and use common sense. Do not overdo it in the beginning. You are not training for a marathon or competing in an Iron Man contest. If you work out too hard or too long the first few times, you risk serious injury to joints, ligaments, and tendons. If you are getting light-headed, dizzy, or gasping for air, then you started out too fast and hard. You can begin with just five minutes, then stretch it to 10 or 15. The body needs time to adjust to this new activity and it needs a resting period afterward. Set a goal to undertake some type of exercise for at least 30 minutes, three or four days a week. Remember it does not have to be one 30-minute block. If you cannot find 30 minutes, then try two 15-minute segments, or three 10-minute segments, or even six 5-minute segments. Remember that 10 minutes is better than zero minutes.

Do not wait until the weekend. Being a weekend warrior is not enough to get you in shape. It only gets rid of stress on the weekend. What do you do with the rest of the stress during the week? It just builds up day after day so that Friday is a day of misery, and you cannot wait until it is over.

To break up the monotony or boredom, try doing different types of exercises on different days. You build up strength and endurance faster if you vary the type of exercise, the repetitions, and the length of each set. I try to change the type of individual exercises I do every day and the overall types every few weeks. There are so many types of exercise you can do to vary the routine. Many good exercise books go into great detail about them.

Take a Day of Rest

When you are just starting out, pay attention to your body and any aches or pains you have. In the beginning, you are going to be sore. Have a day of rest in between exercising days until your body becomes accustomed to the workout. By not resting, you may be overusing the muscles, leading to injuries. Remember that you are putting new demands on your muscles, joints, ligaments, and tendons. Your body must get familiar with the new routine. It also needs time to repair itself. If you are working with weights, do not work the same set of muscles two days in a row. They need a break.

Do not expect to see instant change and benefits. Depending on the activity you choose, it may take a few weeks or a month before you notice improvements. What you will probably notice very quickly is that you will find it easier to get rid of the stress each day and cope with it the next day. Eventually, you will see changes in strength, endurance, attitude, and the way you look.

Keep an Exercise Log

One of the best ways to reach your goals and stick to them is by keeping an exercise log or diary from day one. Jot down an anecdotal record of what you did and for how long a period of time. It does not matter whether it was a five-minute exercise break at work, or a one-hour game of tennis, write it down immediately. If you decided not to exercise, make a note and list the reason why. This feedback can be very enlightening and motivating.

Looking at the log over time shows the progress you have made. You will see how you extended your endurance or built up your strength, and if you have walked or jogged further, increased your repetitions, or increased your pulse rate. If you do not have large blocks of time, and are doing three or four short spurts of activity during a workday, you will have a record of what you are doing to counteract the stress. It will also show you the times you have been lazy or skipped your destressing activities. As you make headway and reach certain goals, reward yourself in some way that is healthy, but do not celebrate by eating a pint of ice cream!

Enlist Support

Discuss your plans and goals with family, friends, co-workers, and your boss. They may even want to work out with you. Be sure to let them know how important this is to you, and what it means to have their support.

If you are planning to exercise before you eat lunch, let your boss know. Discuss the benefits it will bring to you in terms of gaining a better ability to handle stress, and less chance of getting sick. If you approach it as a benefit to your performance and productivity, and how it will help the company, your boss will be much more encouraging, and may even give you some extra time for it.

THREE WAYS TO DESTRESS

There are three major categories of exercise: stretching, strength training, and cardiovascular. Each benefits you in a different way. First, decide what your objective is. Are you looking for cardiovascular endurance? Then you may want to consider aerobic activities, which speeds up the heart, strengthens it, and increases lung capacity. These exercises include moderate to fast walking, jogging, aerobics classes, bicycling, and any exercise that challenges you to move faster than normal. (See Figure 3.3.)

Are you looking to increase your strength? Then you want to consider resistance training. This involves the use of resistance or weights on muscles in order to

FIGURE 3.3   Exercise Quiz

If you are already doing some exercise, take this quiz to get a baseline of how far along you are at this time, and set higher goals.

	Yes	No
I keep a positive attitude about exercise.	——	——
I have made a firm commitment to stay in shape.	——	——
I do some exercise every day, for at least 15 minutes.	——	——
I have created a personal fitness plan with goals.	——	——
I walk instead of driving whenever I can.	——	——
I stretch at least four times per week.	——	——
I do some kind of strength training three times per week.	——	——
I raise my heart rate with aerobics three times per week.	——	——
I play some type of sport once a week.	——	——
I log and monitor my activities and progress.	——	——

build strength and stamina. These exercises include calisthenics, free weights (dumbbells), isometrics, and weight machines.

Are you looking to increase your flexibility? Then look into simple stretching, yoga, and other ancient forms of movement and stretching such as Tai Chi or Qigong. These types will also increase the range of motion of your joints, make you more supple, and they also prevent stiffness and soreness. Stretching will be looked at in more detail in Chapter 5.

The American College of Sports Medicine recommends a combination of all three types of exercise. Cross training of all three provides you with variety and prevents boredom. You must also consider whether you need an instructor for the activity you choose, and what the cost will be.

Warm Up/Cool Down

No matter which type of exercise or activity you pick, it should begin with a warm-up period and end with a period of cooling down. Your body should not go from a state of rest as in a bed or chair, to a sudden burst of activity. If you are planning to undergo an extensive exercise period, you need to prepare your heart, lungs, and muscles for that type of workout. Warming up raises the body's temperature and pumps more blood to the muscles and joints. When your muscles are warmed up they stretch much better. This also helps to prevent injury. This warm-up period may consist of three to five minutes of easy walking, light biking, or some light aerobic activity.

Follow with light stretching for flexibility. You do not want to stretch too hard because the ligaments and tendons are not quite as ready as they will be after you exercise. Stretching should allow you to feel tension in a muscle. Stretch slowly, not in a bouncing or jerking manner. Do not stretch until you feel pain because pain signals that you have gone too far. If you feel pain, you are getting no gain. Remember that you are warming up, not getting ready for a circus act. Take a deep breath before the stretch and exhale as you stretch. Most experts recommend five to 10 seconds on each stretch as a light stretch.

The cooling-down period, after vigorous exercise, allows your heart rate and breathing to return back to normal. You can walk or do aerobics at a lighter pace for another five minutes. This period also includes more vigorous stretching, which is easier since the muscles are warmed up from the activity. Each stretch can be held 10 to 20 seconds. Stretching also helps to prevent soreness.

WALKING AWAY STRESS

Walking is one of the best exercises and destressors because it is easy, and it can be done all the time, indoors or out. It is good for those who hate to exercise. People who begin walking for exercise usually tend to stick with it. They find special, favorite places such as parks and trails to visit. They vary the places from week to week, which keeps them motivated. Age is no excuse. If you are able to walk around your house, you can walk in your neighborhood providing it is safe. You don't need expensive clothing or equipment. All you need are comfortable walking shoes. Remember: Any walking you do, even if it is slow, is better than sitting and doing nothing.

The National Sporting Goods Association estimates that nearly 100 million people walk as a form of exercise, which is more than any other form. Walking improves your cardiovascular system, it has lower impact, and is easier on the body than jogging or running. It is relatively injury-free, and builds muscular strength in the trunk, especially in the back, while it increases your lung capacity. It is a wonderful way to burn calories and control weight. It also clears the mind and acts as a terrific antidote to the fight-or-flight syndrome.

There are more opportunities to squeeze walking into your daily routine than you may realize. Even if the weather is bad, I will walk in my house for 15 to 30 minutes. I will listen to a motivational or learning tape to prevent boredom. If you are going to a store or mall, park further away so you will take more steps. If you are using a parking garage, park further up, so you can walk further. When possible, take the stairs instead of the elevator or escalator, because climbing stairs makes the heart pump more and builds up your leg muscles.

Travel Time Is Walking Time

If you travel frequently by air for your job, as I do, you have an opportunity to walk at the airports. When time allows, I always skip the trains between concourses and walk the distance instead. I can get an extra 15 minutes of walking in at a fast pace. My carry-on luggage is on wheels so I can easily pull it. Pulling the luggage gives me more resistance, works the arms, legs, and heart harder, and gives me a good miniworkout, especially if I have been sitting on the plane for awhile.

When on the road, staying at hotels, I will walk in the surrounding area. If you are going to do this, I suggest always asking the hotel staff how safe the area is around the hotel. They often give me a map and mark off the best route or areas to take. It's an excellent way to see part of a city. If the weather does not cooperate, I often take advantage of the hotel's health club and use the treadmill, bicycle, or pool. If there is none available, I will just walk in the halls. Some of the hotels are so large, you can easily spend 15 minutes exploring them. The carpeting is usually well-padded, so there is less pounding on the body than when walking the streets.

If you spend many hours on an airplane, try not to sit more than an hour without getting up. I will walk up and down the aisle to the furthest restroom, and I will find an area, usually near the back galley, where I can stretch. I never had a flight attendant tell me to sit down, unless the flight was bumpy.

Walking at Work

Think about how long you sit during the day when you are at work. The same rule applies there, too. Try not to sit for more than one hour because your body needs to move around. Constant sitting adds to back strain and muscle tightness in the thighs (the hamstrings). Get up, stretch, and walk around, even if it is only for five minutes. Consider walking before lunch or during your break times. Ask co-workers to walk with you. If practical, go out for a walk around the block during a break. I have a friend who takes coffee breaks by walking up and down a few flights of stairs in his office building. Remember that movement gets rid of the stress, while eating snacks and drinking coffee or soda does not.

Just keep asking yourself, "What can I do to take more steps?" It does not have to be power or speed walking. A casual stroll for 5 to 10 minutes still relieves stress, and a brisk walk is even better. Any walking you do is better than sitting.

Helpful Hints before You Walk

Do not go the cheap route when it comes to buying walking shoes. Find quality walking shoes, not jogging shoes because they are made differently. Be sure they have enough cushioning inside, particularly in the heels to absorb the shock of each step. Always wear or keep a comfortable pair of walking shoes with you. If you are walking outdoors, be especially alert if you wear an audio or headset. Be aware of traffic, people, and dogs. If you are walking at night, wear clothing that can be easily seen or is made with reflective colors. Carry identification with you at all times.

STRENGTHENING YOUR GRIP

Simply defined, strength training is the process of working your muscles through some type of resistance. We most often identify it with the use of weights, whether it be free weights or machines. But, you can also strengthen muscles without weights through activities such as swimming and biking, while at the same time get aerobic benefits.

Strength training or resistance training with weights is a great stress releaser. In particular, it gets rid of feelings of anxiety, anger, nervousness, and depression. At the same time, it increases the strength of muscles, ligaments, and tendons. Strength training increases bone mass, and subsequently prevents injuries, especially as you get older. It also helps with the ease of movement and the extent of motion of the joints. Strength training also helps to rid the body of fat, lose weight, and lowers cholesterol and triglycerides. Calories burn off for a few hours after you have finished the workout. Cardiovascular functions and breathing become more efficient.

People begin losing muscle mass, a process known as atrophy, as early as in their twenties. You may not notice it until age 40, but at some point we all say that we cannot lift what we used to, or cannot go up as many flights of stairs as we did years ago. We feel we do not have the stamina and endurance we once had. Our reaction time and balance begins to decrease. At this point, we are losing bone mass, and the ligaments, tendons, and joints degenerate. We begin to add more fat to the body. But this process can be reversed, to a degree, by strength training.

The beauty of resistance training is that it helps people of all ages. A lot of research on this subject has been done with people at every stage of life. The studies show that no matter how long you have gone without resistance training, your muscles will still respond. You can regenerate muscle mass and bone density, even at 85 years old. Strength training also helps older people with balance.

Some people cringe at the idea of using weights because it takes time and energy, both of which are in short supply before, during, and after the workday. Many find it distasteful to spend the money and take time to drive to a gym. They do not want to wait for a machine, and do not have 60 or 90 minutes to work out. Some people try to solve this by putting complicated machines in their homes. Too many times these machines become like some strange, elaborate, and expensive clothes hanger, collecting dust and taking up space in a room because of lack of use.

Keep It Simple and Light

Working with weights does not have to be very complicated. I am talking about getting rid of stress, not becoming Mr. or Ms. Universe. If you want to get into bodybuilding, that is something else entirely. I just want you to use weights to destress, prevent burnout, and increase your strength and endurance.

You only need a set of hand-held dumbbells, with weights of 5, 10, 15, and 20 pounds to get started. You can add more weight later. Dumbbells are good because they are light, easy to use, and you can do so many different exercises with them. You can also purchase wrap-around ankle weights with a sleeve that enables you to add or subtract little weights to change the resistance. Another great invention are dumbbells that you can fill up with water, which are terrific for taking on business trips.

Resistance bands are lightweight, large, elastic rubber bands that you can use to pull and stretch. You can strength train many different muscles with them. They can be put in a desk drawer and used at work. They readily fit into a suitcase to be taken on trips. Some of them come with a list of descriptive exercises, and the best part is that they are usually $15 or less.

It is not my purpose to give you specific strengthening exercises, so find a good book on weight training at the library or bookstore. Read about how to lift, how often to lift, and how many reps and sets to do. This will enable you to increase your strength in the right manner without risking injury.

Consider the amount of time you realistically can set aside for weights. If you do not have a block of time, consider exercising with them two or three times a day for a shorter period of time. I know people that keep light dumbbells or resistance bands at work, and pull them out when they feel themselves getting stressed. They may use them for only five minutes, but it gets rid of the stress and reenergizes them. A good idea is to use them for another 10 minutes when you get home. You can try another 10 minutes later in the evening.

The point is that you do not want to make weight training such drudgery that you skip it. You do not want to get stressed out over lack of time. Doing two to four short periods of strength training during the day still has the same effect of ridding the body of stress and strengthening the muscles as longer training times do. Remember: It is the total minutes that count. Pretty soon, you will begin to feel less stressed during the workday, plus you will experience increased strength and stamina to deal with the day's events.

MORE CHOICES TO CHECK OUT

There are so many other exercises that are beneficial to us. I am not trying to make anyone into a fitness fanatic, but try to look at it as a healthy antidote to the fight-or-flight syndrome. I want you to keep thinking every day that you have to do something about the buildup of stress hormones. The following exercises are suggested because they are fun, require little or no learning, and are inexpensive. Although they cannot be done at work, unless you have a gym on the premises, they can be done during your lunch time. Remember, it is not so important to set aside a large block of time, as much as it is to think of total minutes spent during the day exercising and destressing.

Jogging or Running

Jogging or running are excellent for your cardiovascular system, as well as your pulmonary system. They are great ways to build endurance and stamina, and are exceptional for burning calories and losing weight.

Sometimes the weather can be challenging to jog or run in. Both forms of exercise are tough on ligaments and tendons of the knees, ankles, and back. A treadmill can solve those problems. Be sure not to skimp on buying a good pair of running shoes with proper cushioning. Cheap, poorly made shoes can only add to your risk of injury and pain.

Biking

Bicycling is one of my personal favorites, but that is because I live in South Florida and can ride almost every day. The downside to biking is the risk you have from traffic and falls. It is excellent for your cardiovascular system. If you have leg problems it is excellent for arthritis, which makes it difficult to put weight on the legs. It is great for overweight people who do not want to jog or run. Physical therapists will tell you it is one of the best exercises for the knee and hip joints, as well as the back. The constant motion of the legs acts as a moving meditation, helping to clear the mind and bring energy to the body.

Biking gets you outdoors, weather permitting, where you can explore a lot of areas you do not normally visit. If the weather allows, consider biking to work (if it is close by), to a store, or to run errands. If you have frequent bad weather days, consider purchasing a stationary bike. They are good, especially for the back, because you sit in a more erect position.

Golfing

Golf is great game for walking exercise, even if it is inter-rupted walking. You can walk up to five miles on an 18-hole course. You may want to consider using the golf cart less and less. In addition, the beautiful courses and surrounding landscape can be very relaxing, even tranquilizing for many. Golf is a great destressor; one of the best!

I often ask my audience members how many of them play golf. Then I ask them how many get frustrated and angry during golf. Many raise their hand. If you have a competitive nature, and get stressed out over the game, I would suggest thinking about your reaction. Interestingly, heart attacks on golf courses are common. Could there be a connection to the anger and rage that some experience on the links? If you react this way, you need to change the way you see the game. If you find that you spend a few hours after the game in an upset and angry state of mind, then do something to get rid of that anger, such as meditation.

Swimming/Water Exercise

When you think of swimming as an exercise, think of the word *safe*, because that is what it is. Since you are moving in water, swimming does not create the jolting wear and tear on the joints of the hips, shoulders, back, or knees. The water helps to relax muscles and gets rid of stress and tension. There is no trauma to the muscles or bones. It is great for middle-aged people and seniors with arthritis, because it increases flexibility and range of motion in the joints. Swimming is an excellent low-impact aerobic exercise.

You may want to look into water aerobics classes that are usually done in waist to shoulder high water. The buoyancy of the water helps to cushion the impact on the bones and muscles. It has very low impact, and is great for older people and those who are overweight. People with injuries find this a great alternative to the hard impact of land aerobics or running.

An Ending Thought

Any time you move faster than normal, with more resistance, in a repetitive fashion, you are burning calories, increasing blood flow, strengthening your body, and eliminating stress. There are movements we can all do that are often not considered exercise, but you still get some of the same benefits. These movements include housework, yard work, dancing to a favorite song, and many hobbies. If you do not want to do the exercises I suggested here or in the next chapters, then do something each day that gets you moving and diverts and clears your mind. The important thing is to get a grip on your stress, and exercise so you can thrive at work each and every day.

4

THE
MIND-BODY CONNECTION

There is an Indian proverb or axiom that says that everyone is a
house with four rooms, a physical, a mental, an emotional and a
spiritual. Most of us tend to live in one room most of the time but,
unless we go into every room every day, even if only to keep it
aired, we are not a complete person.

(Godden, 1989)

Stress can make us feel like the title from the old Broadway play, "Stop the World, I Want to Get Off." Besides affecting our bodies, stress very often clutters our minds putting us on a merry-go-round of obsessive thoughts and worry. Sometimes our minds feel like they will explode. Fortunately, there is an answer to slowing the busy, stressful mind: meditation. Meditation is actually a form of resting or being still that enables us to destress. Meditation is a simple method of destressing without having to exert physical energy. As a matter of fact, you do not have to exert anything; not even your mind. Anyone can do it, including those with limited mobility. The only requirement is breathing. The amazing part of practicing meditation is all the other benefits that come with it. (See Figure 4.1.)

FIGURE 4.1   Benefits of Meditation

Reduces stress and burnout.

Increases overall better health and quality of life.

Lowers blood pressure.

Decreases chance of heart disease.

Decreases pain.

Increases overall happiness.

Enables you to overcome sadness, anxiety, and depression.

Increases focus and concentration.

Enhances problem-solving and decision-making ability.

Increases creativity.

Increases spirituality.

Gain a deeper purpose in life.

Increases compassion, understanding, and love for others.

THE SECRET OF THE AGES

No one can say for sure when meditation first started, but it has been with us since the first days of our earliest ancestors. Some meditated by staring at the stars on clear nights, while others stared at flames of the village fire in the evenings. There are references to meditation in the Bible and in cave drawings. Ancient tribal shamans would enter an altered state or trance while dancing or listening to the sound of drums. From India came the meditative postures of the ancient yogis that spread to China and Tibet. From the teachings of Buddha, who practiced yoga, came the concept of mindful meditation. From the ancient Chinese Taoists came the slow movement meditations. Over time, meditation made its way to the Middle East where it had an effect on Judeo-Christian and Islamic teachings and traditions. Early Christian monks practiced meditation to become closer to God. Early Jewish meditators used mystical Kabbalah to communicate with God. Muslim Sufis, before the time of Mohammed, practiced meditation through a twirling, spinning movement, while praying, to communicate with Allah.

Native Americans were already meditating for centuries before America was discovered. Eastern forms of meditation made their way across the Atlantic with some of the earliest colonists. It has been practiced in the United States ever since, but did not become mainstream, until the 1960s and 1970s. At that time, it was vividly brought to our attention by the Maharishi Mahesh Yogi, whose teachings on Transcendental Meditation (TM) were studied directly by the Beatles and other celebrities, and became a practice of the hippie culture. Transcendental Meditation comes from Hinduism and makes use of a repetitive sound or mantra assigned by a teacher. For years it had been looked on as something done by smiling Maharishis in full-length robes with long beards. At first, many people were skeptical about practicing it because of the incense, mantras, and chanting. Now meditation has become mainstream, and is practiced by over 10 million people in America. Its beneficial effects on the body and mind have been highly studied.

There are many different forms of meditation practiced in the United States, from the Zen Meditation of Buddhist monks, to the Transcendental Meditation (TM) of the Maharishis of India, to the "Relaxation Response" described by Dr. Herbert Benson, a medical doctor from Harvard University. Meditation also includes forms of moving meditation and postures such as yoga, Tai Chi, and ChiGong, which we will discuss in the next chapter.

Why Meditate?

Meditation is not a religion, and it does not ask you to change your own philosophical or religious beliefs. You do not have to be a religious person, although meditation can increase your understanding of religion and bring you closer to God. It does not ask you to give up your values or change your lifestyle. You do not need to join a cult. You do not need a guru to call your own.

The purpose of meditation is to slow and quiet the mind, and in turn, quiet the body. If you can quiet the mind, you can achieve a feeling of peace and tranquility. You gain better control of your thoughts and feelings. It is a method to gain mastery over a thought process, and it teaches you to focus your mind, so that your thoughts are no longer scattered. You temporarily slow down your thinking, and achieve a state of deep relaxation. However, you are still totally conscious of your surroundings. You train your mind by concentrating or focusing on a sound, word, prayer, image, object (such as a candle), nature, or an idea. If you use a word or sound, it is referred to as a mantra.

Sometimes the mind is almost uncontrollable. It can run like a wild stallion, difficult to slow down or rein in. Meditation helps you to be in the present moment. It helps you to deal with the here and now, a practice in Buddhism known as mindfulness. It means being intensely aware of that present moment, and living in that moment.

Meditation liberates your mind from distracting thoughts and brings it to a state of calm. You actually detach yourself from those thoughts and make them diminish. It allows you to expand your consciousness and become aware of thoughts, feelings, and emotions so you may control them better. Meditation strengthens the appreciation of how your mind and body interact. It enables you to remain focused.

People meditate for many different reasons. Some do it to control stress, anger, and negative feelings. Others meditate for its relaxing effect on the body and the tranquil effect on the mind. Some practice meditation for the healing effects it gives. Many meditate for the wisdom and creativity it provides. Some people meditate for a very simple reason: It makes your body and mind immediately feel good. Anyone can meditate, no matter the age.

No matter what the reason, meditation is perfect for people who say they don't have the energy to exercise. It is great for those that are physically unable to exercise. It is a great practice for people who don't have one hour to exercise. All you need is 5 to 20 minutes. Meditation can be done at work, before lunch or during a break, given that you have a relatively quiet place to do it. It is another powerful tool for destressing. Having meditated for the past 11 years, I find it also enhances my exercise, as it gives me the energy to have a great workout. Meditation, coupled together with exercise, gives you a powerful combination to knock out the daily work stress, stop the mind from thinking and worrying, and reenergize you for the next day.

MEDITATION: WHAT IT CAN DO FOR YOU

Dr. Herbert Benson, a Harvard University cardiologist, was the first to conclusively link together the benefits of meditation with Western medicine. He scientifically explained the benefits of meditation that people have been practicing for centuries. His research on practitioners of Eastern Transcendental Meditation (TM) during the 1960s and 1970s was published in his highly respected book, *The Relaxation Response*, originally published in 1975. Benson stated, "Once the data was compiled, we found the facts were incontrovertible. With meditation alone, the TM practitioners brought about striking physiologic responses—a drop in heart rate, metabolic rate, and breathing rate—that I would subsequently label 'the Relaxation Response.' Further research found that meditation also lowered blood pressure for people who had elevated levels" (2000, xvi). His research proved, beyond any doubt, that meditation led to a state of deep relaxation, which he asserted was the perfect antidote for the fight-or-flight syndrome. Meditation counteracts the impact of the stress hormones released in our blood.

Since then, hundreds of articles have appeared in peer-reviewed scientific journals that attest to the wonderful health benefits of meditation. A recent cover story in *Time* magazine proclaimed in its headline, "Millions of Americans . . . practice it every day. Why? Because meditation works" (Stein, 2003). Doctors of Western medicine and science are studying its impact because research has proven its dramatic positive impact on our stress-laden lives. Refer back to the benefits that are listed in Figure 4.1. The research points to the conclusion that people who meditate live longer, happier, and healthier lives. They spend less time being sick, going to doctors, or being confined to hospitals.

The benefits have become so important, that in 2003 Tibetan Buddhist monks, along with the Dalai Lama, met with American neurologists and researchers in behavior medicine at MIT to discuss the medical research on meditation. The conference was sold out and had a large waiting list. Further research and more conferences are in the planning stages. These unprecedented types of meetings between masters of meditation and medical researchers will ensure that the benefits of meditation will continually be explored and described for years to come.

Workplace Benefits

Some of the greatest benefits of meditation exhibit themselves in the workplace. These benefits are greatly enhanced if you can find time to meditate before you leave for work, before lunch, or during breaks. This short investment in time will reap great rewards in your daily performance. You are better prepared to prevent the stress response from happening, or can lessen its effects.

Meditation allows you to keep your attitude up, when everyone else is down. You learn to avoid using negative self-talk. Meditation acts as a buffer between you and self-defeating remarks or behavior. By practicing it, your attitude will become more tolerant of the events that are happening around you. You will not fight the changes that occur, and can better handle the surrounding turbulence. If the outcomes are not positive, you can learn to accept them better, or you will start gathering facts to see how you can change them. As a result, you will feel you are more in control of your own destiny.

Practicing meditation enables you to stay calm when working under pressures of a deadline. You do not react with the same anxiety, stress, or fear that you would if you never meditated. You will not fly off the handle if you are interrupted while trying to get a task or project done. You will be better able to stay in the moment and control your reactions. You will be more resilient to anger. You find you can observe your thoughts so you may calm them.

Because you have learned to focus your mind through meditation, you are able to concentrate better. You can block out background noise in the workplace. Clamor that disturbed you before is no longer a distraction. You become less prone to making costly errors. You have more stamina to ward off the fatigue and have a deeper attention span. As a result, you are more productive. Since your mind is clearer, it enables you to cut through the clutter that goes with making difficult decisions.

Your thoughts are less scattered and chaotic. I like to use the analogy of the spray nozzle placed on the end of the hose. You can change to a spray of water that scatters in all directions or you can switch to a focused stream that comes out in one hard and fast direction. This focused thinking enhances your creativity. You can pay greater attention to minor details. If you are in a job where creativity is critical, such as advertising, marketing, or sales, meditation greatly enhances your ability to come up with new ideas. Creativity seems to bubble up from a place deep within your mind. You are uncapping a potential you never knew you had.

Meditation allows you to work better with people. You can build relationships easier because you have become more accepting of yourself and of others. You learn to have compassion and caring for others. Imagine becoming more patient of your co-workers, and more tolerant of their weaknesses and mistakes. Meditation enables you to forgive people for the wrongs they have directed at you. You may even practice random acts of kindness to those you have disliked or argued with for years.

MEDITATION GUIDELINES

You can meditate any time it feels right, but it is especially effective when you are most stressed. It is great to meditate before you become engaged in some busy or stressful period of work or networking with people. It makes you more alert and full of energy. I like to meditate just before I begin speaking because it keeps me calm, focused, and centered.

When to Meditate

Many teachers of meditation suggest meditating just after waking in the morning because this is the time when your subconscious mind is the most open. Your body has rested and is reenergized. It is a perfect time to clear the mind so you can concentrate on the day's work ahead. You can fill the subconscious mind with positive thoughts and set the tone for the day. Unfortunately, in this hectic world, with dual-career families and single parents, this may be unrealistic for some people. There just is no time.

Another time to meditate is right before going to sleep, especially if you have problems turning off your thoughts. This enables you to calm your mind and clear out the worries from the day and the concerns of tomorrow. It helps you to enter into a more peaceful and deeper sleep, and does wonders for your energy level the next day.

Some people perform three or four minimeditations a day, 5 or 10 minutes each. I personally like the shorter meditations, especially during a high-pressure day. I have found that short meditation is much better than no meditation. I also use longer meditations when I have the time, particularly on an airplane.

Others meditate once or twice a day for 15 to 20 minutes. Those that have meditated for a while will often extend it to a half hour or more. Try different time frames and see which gives you the most benefit. When you find the time that is right for you, try to schedule it in the same time every day. Time pressures, free time, and lifestyle will often dictate which time may fit the best into your life.

Be careful not to meditate immediately after you eat because the digestive process interferes with the response you want. Do not meditate when you are exhausted, because it will not reenergize you. If you are extremely tired, you may just fall asleep, which is what your body needs the most at that moment.

As with exercising, start out slow, meditating just a few minutes, until you become familiar with the process. I remember the first time I meditated, it was only for 5 minutes. It seemed like an eternity, as my mind wandered like an excited, wild monkey on a tree filled with bananas. Try 5 minutes for the first week, add 2 minutes the next week, and increase it another 2 minutes the week after. If you have time, work your way up, incrementally, to 15- or 20-minute sessions. If you can do that twice a day, it would be more beneficial. But remember, once a day is better than not at all.

The important thing is to make a commitment to meditating on a regular basis. In other words, set aside time each day, even if it is for a short meditation. The more frequently you meditate, the greater the rewards you will reap. As you progress, the benefits will increase and get stronger. It is like exercising a muscle. The more you do it, the stronger it gets, and the better you will feel.

Where to Meditate

You can meditate just about anywhere. Pick quiet or peaceful spots that enable you to focus your mind. You don't want too many distractions. Any closed room in the house will do. Be sure you are in a location with a good supply of fresh air. When the temperature is right, I open the windows.

I also meditate on my back patio. The sound of birds in my yard is very peaceful and relaxing. Balconies, decks, and patios are great, as long as there is not too much noise. Any garden, park, or group of flowers, plants, or trees are ideal for meditation. They create a wonderful, soothing mind-set.

I have a friend who meditates at work, behind his desk, at

the end of the day, to calm down. He feels this helps him handle the ride home, which is on a busy freeway during rush hour. Other people meditate at work behind their desk instead of taking coffee breaks. Some have told me that they ask not to be disturbed for those 10 minutes, and will even put a sign on their door. I realize this is not practical for everybody, as some do not have an office or desk.

A seminar participant, who is a very busy small-business owner, in a high-stress environment, told me that he goes to a park every day during his lunch hour. He meditates for 15 minutes, then eats lunch. He turns off his cell phone because he does not want the serene mood to be broken. He has informed his staff he does not want to be located unless the business is on fire. He said in 15 years of doing this, there has never been an emergency that could not wait until he returned to the office. He feels recharged for the afternoon.

Meditation can be practiced on airplanes and in hotel rooms. Some people go into churches and synagogues to meditate. Many people find a beautiful and quiet outdoor spot. Do it when and where it feels right. Do it when you need it.

Make It Enjoyable

If you make meditation enjoyable, you are more apt to continue to practice it. If it is not enjoyable, you will quickly give it up, losing a wonderful way to destress. Too many people try to become perfect meditators right from the start. When they discover their mind is wandering, they may try too hard to prevent it. When they realize they cannot stop the wandering, they become frustrated. They begin to think they are not good at it, and try forcing or controlling their method and response.

Meditation is supposed to be an enjoyable experience, not

one that aggravates you or adds more stress to your life. Your mind is going to wander because it is a busy place. This is a natural process that the mind undergoes. It doesn't mean you are meditating the wrong way. Thoughts will enter your mind; some of them not so pleasant. No matter what the thoughts are, it is normal for them to be there. You will feel a variety of emotions and moods. This is common; do not fight it. Do not be critical of yourself. Lighten up! Just tell yourself it is okay, and return to your focus.

Talk to Yourself

Our minds are incredibly powerful. We have known for years that we can change our lives simply by altering our thought process and what we say to ourselves. Your body hears all the self-talk you tell your mind, and it responds either positively or negatively. Since it is good for your health, you might as well create a habit of telling yourself positive thoughts and statements. An affirmation is simply a positive statement that you tell yourself again and again. The purpose of an affirmation is to help you accomplish a specific result or goal. It also helps you change your mind-set, from negative to positive. You can use affirmations any time of the day or any place.

For example, if you want to quit smoking, constantly telling yourself "I quit smoking" can help you achieve that goal. If you want to lose weight, you can tell yourself, "I am slim." You can use affirmations in many other ways. A salesperson can repeatedly tell herself, "I will close the deal." If you are going for a job interview, you can tell yourself, "I will do great" or "I am relaxed." If you are giving a presentation, you can say, "I am peaceful/calm/relaxed." I use affirmations to pump myself up before a keynote speech in front of a large audience. I also use them to stay calm in situations like traffic jams or while negotiating a contract. Affirmations can help you to stay relaxed in difficult and stressful situations.

A positive mind-set can do wonders for your body. Having positive thoughts can increase your body's ability to fight disease and heal itself. By constantly affirming that an injury is healing, or a sickness is going away, you can cause the body to respond in a positive way and shorten the healing process. Constantly affirming with positive thoughts is a way of adding to the work of your doctor and speeding up recovery. A few months ago, I badly hurt my back lifting something. I used a constant stream of affirmations such as "my back feels good" or "my back is strong." I repeated it so much, it became like a mantra. It was amazing how quickly my back healed.

Seeing Is Believing

Visualization is using your imagination and seeing yourself in a particular situation that you want to happen. You imagine yourself as already being or living in that condition or situation. Many athletes have used visualization to see themselves in competition, performing to perfection. It gives them a competitive edge.

Your imagination is incredibly powerful and can help you see and achieve what you want. It enables you to reach your goals. There is a phrase used by many motivational speakers. I don't believe anyone knows who first used it. It states, "If you can see it, you can believe it, and achieve it." By visualizing yourself in a new job, house, or car, it moves you toward achieving that goal. We become what we see and think about. Your mind locks on to that image and each day you do the things necessary to make it a reality. You become like a heat-seeking missile moving toward its target.

Even more important, you can use visualization to improve your health and get rid of stress. Just as you can use affirmations to improve health, your mind can visualize the body's process of improving health. Your subconscious mind is most open to visualization the first half hour after awakening, and the time just before you fall asleep. This is a great time to visualize your body getting stronger or healing any injuries or disease. It is a time to see yourself filled with boundless energy. It is a time to visualize yourself staying calm and relaxed in stressful situations.

At the same time, you can say affirmations aloud and to yourself to reinforce what you have visualized. I like to use affirmations about my health, mentally visualizing different parts of my body and affirming to myself how healthy they are. This works especially well in self-healing.

Visualization is an integral part of the meditative process. A wonderful time to visualize is just after you have meditated. This powerful combination has a potent impact on the mind. First, clear or quiet the mind through meditation, thus relaxing the body. Next, visualize an outcome that you want to take place. Visualizing a goal or situation has a more powerful effect after meditating than just visualization alone.

Dr. Herbert Benson traveled to northern India to study Tibetan monks who were in exile. His travels revealed how powerful the mind-body connection is. He found that these monks could live at high altitudes, in freezing temperatures, dressed in only small loincloths and remained warm. They accomplished this through a type of heat-producing meditation. They could actually dry wet, cold sheets from the heat of their bodies. At first, they would meditate to quiet the mind. Next, they would visualize a fire or heat that warmed their bodies.

Dr. Benson began to teach his patients this "two-step

process" that the monks utilized. "First, you evoke the Relaxation Response and reap its healthful rewards. Then, when your mind is quiet, when focusing has opened a door in your mind, visualize an outcome that is meaningful to you. . . . Whatever your goal, these two steps can be powerful, allowing anyone to reap the benefits of the Relaxation Response and take advantage of a quiet mind to rewire thoughts and actions in desired directions" (Benson, 2000, xi).

BREATHING: THE LIFE FORCE

In many ancient traditions and philosophies, the breath is linked to the life force and source of all energy within us. Many types of meditation around the world are linked to breathing. The ancient masters of Chinese meditation, such as Tai Chi and ChiGong, learned to control their breathing. By doing this, they learned ways to control other bodily functions such as heartbeat and blood pressure. Through breathing, they could control the flow of energy into the body. Since they believed in the breath as being the source of all energy, they also believed it determined physical and mental health. They learned to direct the flow of energy to different parts of the body where it was needed and used for self-healing.

Breathing is critical to our health and vitality. You can only live a few minutes without it. It is what gives us energy, creativity, motivation, and wisdom. So often we hear the advice, when under stress or when we are angry, to take a few deep breaths. It is a great antidote for bringing calm to the mind and body.

We saw in Chapter 3 that the more oxygen we allow to the cells, the more energized we become. Breathing properly overcomes stress and relaxes the chest and rib cage muscles.

It decreases fatigue and builds stamina. Breathing is not something that is to be taken lightly. The teachers of meditation work on their breathing throughout their life. The focus on the breath, known as conscious breathing, is one of the building blocks of meditation. It is actually one of the most basic forms of meditation.

Bad Breath/Good Breath

During my stress management seminars, I frequently ask my audiences, "Do you know how to breathe?" They often give me a look of astonishment or laugh. The fact is most people do not realize that they are not breathing properly. For many, each breath is shallow and restricted, nowhere near the capacity it should be. If you are not getting enough oxygen, you are not full of energy and you frequently get sleepy. You have less tolerance for stressors. The stressors in turn cause you to breathe shallower. It's a de-energizing cycle.

Here's a little experiment you can try: Stand, sit, or lie down with your back straight. Put one hand on your stomach, partly on the navel and just below it. Place the other hand on your chest. Take the deepest breath you can. Which part was raised during the inhalation? Was it your chest or your stomach? If your chest was raised the most, then you are not breathing from the stomach or from the diaphragm. If your stomach expanded and the chest did not move, or slightly fell, then you are breathing properly.

Take another deep breath and focus on your shoulders. If your shoulders move up during inhalation, again you are not breathing properly. If you are breathing from the stomach or diaphragm, the shoulders should not rise. With a little practice you can easily perfect this technique.

When you breathe from the abdomen, you take in much

more oxygen, which circulates throughout the body. Upon inhalation, you expand the stomach muscles and the muscles in the rib cage, and you lower the diaphragm. As the belly rises, it looks as if the stomach is actually inflated with air. Upon exhalation, the diaphragm moves in an upward direction, and your stomach and rib cage move inward. Many athletes, actors, professional speakers, and singers have wisely learned the benefits of abdominal breathing or diaphragmatic breathing. Try it and you will find it de-stresses and reenergizes you.

Breathing Exercise

Many forms of Eastern meditation teach the practice of proper breathing. From Hatha Yoga comes the breathing practice sometimes known as three-part breathing, of which there are a number of variations. I learned it in the first meditation class I took, and have used it for many years with wonderful results every time. It is a wonderful way to relax the mind and body before meditation. Be sure to sit in a comfortable chair and close your eyes.

In the first part of the exercise, we completely exhale all the air in our lungs. Once we have rid our lungs of every bit of air, we take a long slow deep breath from 8 to 10 seconds, completely filling the lungs. In part two, we hold that breath for one to three seconds. In part three, we completely exhale every ounce of air again for 10 seconds. Try it two or three times and feel the results. Expand it later to four or five repetitions. It brings a real feeling of peace and relaxation. Not only can it be used before meditation, but this is an exercise we can do at home, at work, or just about anywhere. I use it frequently, always before stretching, exercising, meditating, or when I need some quick energy. It serves as an instant recharge technique.

Breath Counting

A great method to begin meditation is by breath counting. This is very simple, and anyone can do it. All you need is a comfortable chair in a quiet place. It is a good way to focus your mind on the breath and develop your sense of concentration. It is a wonderful method to learn the discipline of doing one thing at a time. It sounds very easy, but the difficult part is to keep focusing and counting, as the mind wanders. It takes some practice to get good at it.

First, take a few slow, deep breaths or use the three-part breath described previously. Then begin counting to yourself as you breathe, with your eyes closed. Focus only on counting the breath, and nothing else. Different practices state that you should only count to a certain number, such as 5 or 10, and start over, while other methods say to just keep counting for a certain period of time, such as 15 minutes.

Most masters say to breathe through your nose, although some say it does not matter. Some teachers tell you to count each inhalation and each exhalation, while others tell you only to count as you exhale. Try either way and see which one you prefer. Always notice the pause between inhalation and exhalation. If your mind wanders, and it will, don't let it bother you. Just go back to gently and softly counting. You will be amazed what 5 to 10 minutes of this does to reenergize you. An alternate method, that I use, consists of focusing on my belly and counting each expansion and contraction as I breathe. It is just a different point of focus, but the results are the same.

Breath counting or belly focusing is something that can be done for a few minutes at home, at work, on a quiet airplane ride, or anyplace where there are no loud distractions. With breath counting and three-part breathing, you have already begun to meditate.

THREE METHODS TO MELLOW MINDFULNESS

There is no one best meditation to practice. If a teacher tells you (or tries to sell you) that there is only one true path to enlightenment, run the other way. There are literally hundreds of meditations from which to choose. Select one or two techniques that best fit you, and that feel and work the best. You can attend a class, and be taught a particular technique. If you don't like that technique, then seek out others. You will know it was the right technique for you if it was a pleasant experience, and it left you relaxed and reenergized. If you feel better than before you meditated, then you know you are practicing it correctly.

How to Meditate

The important thing is to find a comfortable sitting position where you can totally relax. If you choose to use a chair, be sure the back is straight, and the seat is firm. A desk chair at the office will work well. Your feet should touch the floor. Place your hands on your lap in a comfortable position. You can also choose to sit on a cushion on the floor, with your back straight, although some people say this is not good for their back. You will discover which one feels best.

Close your eyes. Let your whole body go limp. This can be achieved through what is called progressive relaxation. Start at the head and slowly relax all the muscles, working your way down to the feet. Visualize all your muscles letting go of the tension and becoming soft. Let your body melt into the chair. Notice if there is still any tension or tightness anywhere, or if some part of the body does not feel comfortable. Focus on relaxing that tension or shifting your weight so you are totally relaxed. Next, become aware of your breath. Use three to five deep abdominal breaths to further relax you.

Let's look at some other meditations that I have personally used, but more important have worked for millions of others.

The Relaxation Response

Dr. Herbert Benson's research led him to conclude that in order to achieve the benefits of meditation, and elicit what he calls the "Relaxation Response," you must have the following four components to be successful.

First, the location of meditation must be in a quiet area without distractions. This makes the practice easier. Second, you must make use of a constant stimulus such as a sound, word, phrase, or object. Concentration on breathing is very helpful. It allows you to focus on the repetition of the sound or word. Third, you must have a passive attitude. If other thoughts enter the mind, which is normal, just disregard them. Don't make judgments. Go back to your focus. Fourth, you need to be in a comfortable position. Sitting is better than lying down, as you may fall asleep. You want to be as relaxed as possible (Benson, 2000).

I have used this method thousands of times over the years, and find it easy and useful. I have practiced it for as little as 5 minutes, and as much as 30 minutes. It's basic, simple, and gets the proper response every time.

I focus on the breath, and every time I exhale, I usually say the word "one," which is the way Dr. Benson suggested in his original 1975 book. You can substitute whatever word has meaning to you. Sometimes, I will use the word "strong" or say "no pain." This works as affirmations and really energizes me or decreases pain. Sometimes I will focus on an object such as a candle or on a part of nature like a flower or a lake nearby my home. Other objects that have spiritual, religious, or personal meaning are also potent. Here are Dr. Benson's six steps in more detail:

1. Sit quietly in a comfortable position.
2. Close your eyes.
3. Deeply relax all your muscles, beginning at your feet and progressing up your face. Keep them relaxed.
4. Breath through your nose. Become aware of your breathing. As you breathe out, say the word, "one," silently to yourself. For example, breathe in. . .out, "one"; in. . .out, "one"; etc. Breathe easily and naturally.
5. Continue for 10 to 20 minutes. You may open your eyes to check the time, but do not use an alarm. When you finish, sit quietly for several minutes, at first with your eyes closed and later with your eyes opened. Do not stand for a few minutes.
6. Do not worry about whether you are successful in achieving a deep level of satisfaction. Maintain a passive attitude and permit relaxation to occur at its own pace. When distracting thoughts occur, try to ignore them by not dwelling on them and return to repeating "one." With practice, the response should come with little effort. Practice the technique once or twice daily, but not within two hours after any meal, since the digestive processes seem to interfere with the elicitation of the Relaxation Response (2000).

Walking Meditation

Walking Meditation or Zen Walking is an incredible stress-reducing combo because you get physical exercise, with all its benefits, while at the same time, you obtain the benefits of focusing and clearing your mind through meditation. If you want to feel both physically invigorated and mentally relaxed, try it. It's been around for thousands of years. I practice this when I walk my dog in the morning or evening. The only problem that throws off my concentration is when he stops.

Find a peaceful place to walk, preferably outdoors, in a park or where nature is present. First, walk mindfully at your normal pace. Notice the sights, sounds, and smells of the outdoors. Next, begin focusing on each breath, each body movement, and every step. After you have walked for a few minutes, try matching the rhythm of your steps with your breath. This will vary, depending on what rate of speed you are walking or how deep you are breathing. Once you start matching, keep the pace the same and focus on it. You can walk at a slow pace of two or three steps per each inhalation and each exhalation, or at a quicker pace of six steps for a every inhalation, and every exhalation. This meditation is really exhilarating. It gives you the cardiovascular, energizing effect of the walk, while at the same time it unfogs your mind. I have found that it provides great focus, concentration, and creativity.

Universal Light of Healing

This meditation type is one I use for healing any kind of sickness or pain. It is a two-part meditation, just as the one practiced by the monks studied by Dr. Benson. The secondary focus is on a healing light. As usual, begin by sitting, getting comfortable, relaxing, and breathing properly. Begin meditating using the Benson method or one that works best for you.

After you have achieved a state of deep relaxation, use your imagination to visualize a brilliant white light shining from the heavens on you. This universal light contains all that is positive in the world, and has the ability to heal sickness and pain. If you like, see the light as coming from God. Direct this light, with its positive energy, to the area where the sickness or pain is. Notice its ability to get rid of the stress and any other negative feelings you may have within your life. See the light healing that part of the body that needs it. Visualize the organ being healed or the pain diminishing. See the light speeding up your recovery. Imagine that light entering your body, staying deep within you, and continually healing you. After this meditation, it is easy to conjure up this visual image to continue the positive thoughts, feelings, and healing.

In the course of a chapter, it is difficult to communicate what meditation truly is, and what it can do for you. I have barely scratched the surface. You have to practice it to understand it and realize the benefits. If you make the commitment to practice it, only then will you realize how it can impact stress, nurture happiness, bring you peace, and change your life. Only then will you know what millions before you have learned. I have given you only the starting point for a wonderful, meaningful journey. That journey begins with the first steps. Begin taking them now. In the next chapter we will look at five other ways to destress, including other forms of movement meditation.

5

DESTRESSING TOOLS FOR MIND, BODY, AND SPIRIT FITNESS

This chapter is an overview of five types of mind and body exercises that will help you get a grip on stress. Each has its own methodology and philosophy. Some have different strengths than others. All of the exercises complement each other. All are designed to bring together the mind, body, and spirit, so that you will have a much more energetic, healthier, and less stressful life. As you read it, keep an open mind. After reading it, your journey may have just begun. As you begin to research more information, look at videos, or take classes, you will find yourself on a fascinating trek that will educate, enlighten, and heal you.

STRETCHING FOR DESTRESSING

Rob is a construction foreman for a company that lays cable. He spends most of his days standing and overseeing his crew. He must be out there in all kinds of weather. The job is stressful because a digging error by his workers can cause a severing of electric, telephone, water, or gas lines. For years he suffered from lower back stiffness and pain. As he entered his fifties, Rob noticed that the pain became worse. He would constantly pop aspirin all day to relieve the problem. At the end of the day, Rob would go home sapped of energy, and lay down before and after dinner. The problem became so acute, he thought he would have to quit his well-paying job and find other work.

After a visit to a neurologist and subsequent x-rays and a CAT scan, Rob learned there was nothing organically wrong to cause the pain. The doctor sent him to a physical therapist to learn how to stretch and strengthen the back. Within days, he noticed an immediate improvement. His back began to relax, and the pain dissipated. Rob realized the constant standing and the job stress were creating the problem. Now he stretches his back each morning, just after a hot shower. He practices the exercises the therapist taught him with devout discipline. He also takes an exercise mat with him each day, and stretches on the back of his truck when his back begins to tighten and cause pain. Rob's crew teases him, but they have seen an improvement in his attitude and that has been good for everyone. Rob has definitely improved the quality of his life through this stretching regimen.

Stretching can be a solution to many aches and pains. Many people who begin an exercise program put most of their efforts into aerobic activities or strength training. But, there is one other component of being fit that is often overlooked: stretching. Stretching is absolutely critical to maintaining a healthy body and getting rid of stress.

The Benefits of Stretching

The benefits of stretching are many. Stretching enables you to move better, with a wider range of motion, in turn improving your flexibility. By having greater range of motion, there is less chance of injuring yourself when you exercise.

Stretching enables you to strengthen ligaments and tendons, and makes your joints stronger and more efficient. It also improves the circulation to the muscles, joints, and connective tissue. When you are stressed, muscles become tightened. If you sit or stand all day, your back muscles become short, tight, and stiff, often creating pain and discomfort. Stretching allows you to get rid of those tight muscles, relieving stress and tension in the body. After stretching, you actually walk more erect. And you feel better, which has a positive impact on the mind.

Do It Almost Anywhere

Stretching is great because you do not need any equipment to do it, except a floor mat for some of the stretches. I use a mat for my back and hamstring stretches at home. Stretching can be done at home, at work, and on airplanes. Many stretches can be done in a seat or standing up. It does not take much time or interrupt your work for very long. If you work in an office environment, think about how many times during the day that you have a free minute. If you are sending or receiving a fax, or downloading, printing, or copying, you can get up and stretch. You can stretch before lunch and during breaks. When other people see you stretching they will ask you about it, and may want to participate along with you.

I even stretch at frequent flyer lounges at the airport. The receptionists often know me and expect me to stretch. Sure, I get strange looks from other frequent flyers, but these are usually tense people with tight muscles. They are often drinking alcohol and coffee, adding to the stress in their body, while I am relaxing my muscles. I do not care if they stare, because I will probably never see those people again. Interestingly, on more than one occasion, I have had people ask me what I was doing. Some joined in and did stretches with me.

If you are on the phone frequently, use a headset. I am constantly on the phone and found this does wonders for preventing stiffness in the neck and shoulders. It also gives you the freedom to stand up and stretch while talking. Plus, your voice sounds more energetic and dynamic if you are standing and moving. This is a real edge if you are in sales and customer service.

You do not have to warm up before you stretch, as long as you use a lighter stretch of 5 to 10 seconds for each one. Again, think of doing short periods of stretching through-out the workday. When muscles get tight or start to hurt, take a break, and perform some stretches. Do not be afraid to stand and stretch every hour or 90 minutes. It will wake you up, and you become more productive. If you drive long distances for your job, as many sales reps do, stretching is a good way to keep your eyelids from getting heavy while on the road. If I am driving a long distance to speak at a convention, I take a restaurant or bathroom break, and always find a way to get in five minutes of stretches.

Simple stretching will not increase your cardiovascular endurance. It will not give you huge muscles or increase strength by leaps and bounds, and stretching will not help you lose much weight. You must use weight resistance and do aerobics to get those benefits. But, it will stretch and lengthen the muscles, which is another perfect anti-dote for the tensing and shortening that our muscles undergo when we are under stress. In addition, it does have a refreshing and energizing effect, and creates a more tranquil state of mind.

A Few Pointers

Some of the following points I mentioned in Chapter 3, but they are worth repeating. Stretch gently, especially as you just start out. Make it a smooth stretch with no bouncing motion. Inhale before the stretch and exhale during it. Close your eyes and use visualization. Focus on the muscle and where it is being stretched. Do mindful stretching, meaning think of nothing but the process you are performing. Visualize the muscle stretching and becoming loose. Get in the habit of stretching at least once a day. There are hundreds of different stretches, which are beyond the scope of this book. Again, there are a good number of books available on the topic.

PILATES

One of the latest crazes to hit the exercise market is the Pilates-based technique. What may seem like a new idea has actually been around for about 90 years. Joseph Pilates created the exercise system in Germany in the early 1900s. Because his body was weakened from rickets, he developed the exercises when he was a teenager to give him greater strength and ward off other diseases. Pilates began developing a system of pulleys and springs for resistance, strength, and flexibility.

Pilates understood the mind-body connection long before most others. He believed that the mind controls the body and its performance. Pilates brought his philosophy and method to the United States in 1926, where he opened a studio in New York. Ballet dancers immediately embraced the system. George Balanchine became a follower, and he commissioned Pilates to help injured ballet dancers regain their stamina.

The Benefits of Pilates

The basic philosophy of Pilates-based exercise is that the body is out of balance and the exercises will put the body back into equilibrium. The system is designed with specific exercises that stretch and strengthen the body. Many exercises are designed to target muscles that are weak and underused, such as the lower back, stomach, and hamstrings. The beginning exercises take place on a floor mat. More advanced exercises use equipment to develop muscle strength. Exercises are done slowly with a focus on one muscle at a time. The workout places a strong emphasis on breathing, visualization, and the mind-body connection. Much importance is placed on the spiritual as well as the physical well-being. The mind is used to create a meditative state. As a result, the exercises aid in releasing stress, anger, and depression. In addition to stretching and strengthening muscles, the exercises are wonderful for balance and posture.

Pilates-based exercise incorporates specific breathing exercises into the regimen. Great emphasis is placed on the correct way to breathe for each exercise. You are taught to breath deeply, and exhale as you put in the most effort. The deep breathing increases your lung capacity and the amount of oxygen transported to the cells. It reenergizes the body.

TAI CHI

Tai Chi is an ancient form of exercise based on the Chinese philosophy of Taoism. It was originally a form of martial arts dating back between 1,500 and 2,000 years. Taoist and

Buddhist monks practiced Tai Chi as a form of exercise and self-defense. It is closely related to ChiGong (see next section).

The word *tai* means great, while the word *chi* or *Qi* refers to the vital energy, vitality, or the life force inside of us. There is no direct English translation of the word. It flows through all living organisms, and is often referred to as the energy of the universe. In China and its neighbors, the concept of chi is widely acknowledged and taken for granted. The practice of Tai Chi allows us to find that great, special life force or energy that exists within each of us.

In ancient Chinese medicine, one cannot separate the mind from the body. Chinese medicine teaches that when the flow of chi is disrupted in the body, it leads to sickness and disease. When we are under stress, that flow of energy or life force is cut off. Tai Chi brings the flow of energy back.

Keep an Open Mind

If you are reading about chi for the first time, you may be cynical or doubt the concept. It is not widely used in the West. If you want to see that it truly exits within you, then I suggest experiencing it for yourself, at least once, through either Tai Chi or ChiGong. Once you feel the power of chi, as I have, you will realize why so many practice it in the East. You will want to learn and use it on a regular basis. You will also learn why it is a wonderful antidote for stress.

Tai Chi sometimes has been called "moving meditation." It looks similar to a slow motion martial arts or a Kung Fu regimen. By using a series of slow, prescribed movements and deep regular breaths, you relax the body and let go of anger, tension, anxiety, and fear. As you move, your mind is focused strictly on the movements and breath. This focus clears the mind. When the mind is still, it calms and recharges the body.

It is estimated that just under one-fourth of the world's population practices Tai Chi. The reason for its growing rise in popularity is due to its stress-lowering benefits, and that it makes you so relaxed. People who practice it claim it is the best exercise they ever have done. It is easy to learn and can be practiced by just about everyone. People in wheelchairs, depending on their condition, can often practice Tai Chi. Senior citizens love it. Because it is strictly made up of fluid movements, there is no jarring impact on the body. The best part is that it can be done at work before lunch or during breaks in order to destress and reenergize. Classes are frequently offered throughout the community, in gyms, schools, and hospitals.

The Benefits of Tai Chi

When you practice Tai Chi, it is almost as though you open a pressure valve and let out all the stress that has built up. The slow, choreographed movements create a sense of deep relaxation. The energy, or chi, is released throughout the body, giving you greater inner strength and tranquility. Now you have the energy and motivation to begin the new day in a refreshed and energized manner.

The graceful movements in Tai Chi are grouped in a specific patterned sequence known as a *form*. The forms are done in the exact same order each time. The movements are performed from a standing position, extensively utilizing the trunk muscles. This pumps more blood throughout the body, improving the heart and circulatory system. The breathing pattern used during the movements improves the capacity and efficiency of the lungs, allowing greater oxygen flow to the cells.

Tai Chi is instrumental in improving muscularskeletal strength and flexibility. By strengthening ligaments and tendons, it aids in giving us a fuller range of motion at the joints. It strengthens the joints and brings more fluid to them, keeping them lubricated. Many practitioners claim it prevents osteoporosis. The exercises have no negative impact on arthritis. It is also a great exercise for improving balance, and helps to prevent falls and injuries. These are some of the reasons seniors love the regimen, but it is beneficial to people of all ages.

CHIGONG

Harry is a senior vice president for a telephone company. His job often puts him into situations of dealing with the media and city and county government officials. As a result, he is on call 24/7. When service goes out, he is constantly being hounded by media people who want answers. They want to know what went wrong, and when things will be fixed. Sometimes he has to go out in the middle of the night to deal with problems. This puts his family life under great duress.

For Harry, the constant phone calls and stress, and the harassment after hours at home resulted in the classic symptoms of burnout discussed in Chapter 2. He experienced neck spasms, headaches, pain between the shoulder blades, lower back pain, and aching knees. He started to get heart palpitations. He was in a constant state of fatigue. Harry was becoming an emotional wreck.

On an airplane flight to the state capitol to meet with politicians and lobbyists, he read a magazine article about ChiGong. He remembered he once had a Chinese American neighbor who practiced it in his backyard. He used to think it looked and sounded weird, but he knew his neighbor to be the most calm, relaxed person he ever met, although this gentle man had a stressful job as a NASA engineer.

Harry did a little research, and learned that there were courses being offered for ChiGong at the local community college. His enrollment in the class turned out to be a significant life-changing experience. He learned how to breathe, meditate, move, and heal his body. ChiGong became the perfect remedy for his physical and emotional state. He was able to alleviate all the pain, get his heart back into normal rhythm, and reenergize himself. Harry learned how to focus on the important crises and not lose control and react with fear or anger. He can now cope with the stress and pressure and has turned back from that dangerous road to burnout. He knows he will make it to retirement, which is only six years away.

ChiGong or Qigong dates back more than 3,000 years. The word *Gong* means work, so the term *ChiGong* means the work of the energy in your body. It is considered one of the four pillars of ancient Chinese medicine, with the others being massage, acupuncture, and herbal medicine. In China, ChiGong is practiced every day by millions of people. ChiGong is known for its powerful ability to unblock energy and to self-heal. Yet, it is not as popular as Tai Chi in the West.

Many scholars of traditional Chinese medicine believe ChiGong is the basis for Tai Chi, as many of the exercises are similar. However, many ChiGong exercises are not found in Tai Chi. Tai Chi is a continual moving meditation from a standing position. ChiGong exercises are performed in a standing, sitting, or lying position. Many of the exercises are slower than those of Tai Chi. They are more of a meditative posture.

The Benefits of ChiGong

As with Tai Chi, ChiGong's emphasis is on the interfacing of movement, breathing, and mental focus and imagery. Since ChiGong is a form of meditation, it triggers many of the same physical, mental, and spiritual responses as those discussed in Chapter 4. There is a known change in brain chemistry, which positively impacts the entire nervous system. ChiGong aids in cleansing the body and eliminating wastes. It also has been proven to increase the amount of immune cells in our system, thus speeding the healing process. Chinese hospitals recommend that cancer patients practice ChiGong in addition to standard treatments such as radiation and chemotherapy. American doctors and the National Institutes of Health are seriously studying the health benefits of both ChiGong and Tai Chi.

There are over 1,000 exercises in ChiGong, all designed to bring health to the mind, body, and spirit. The abdominal breathing exercises are designed to open the mind and body to a powerful flow of chi. Other stretching and movement exercises are designed to cleanse organs and purify and circulate the chi. Some exercises are combined with producing quiet healing sounds in order to get rid of toxins in the mind and body. All practitioners agree that ChiGong brings peace and harmony to the mind and spirit, while creating a healthy, energetic body.

Once you learn the exercises, they can be done anywhere. You only need enough room to stand and stretch. Like the other destressing exercises previously mentioned, they are ideal to perform at work before lunch or during a break. You can perform many of the postures and movements in about 10 minutes. You do not need to take a class to learn the exercises. I perform the full regimen of exercises at home following a video, which helps me to perform them correctly.

When traveling, I perform an abbreviated version from memory in a hotel room.

YOGA

Robin was a chef in an exclusive restaurant in San Diego. She worked in a fast-paced, high-stress environment. As she approached her forties, she began getting a pain that started in her left hip and ran down her left leg. Robin never paid too much attention to her health, which was always pretty good, and she would usually work through any discomfort she felt. But, lately the pain was getting worse and was unrelenting. It finally forced her to see a doctor. After meeting with an orthopedic specialist and having a round of tests, she was diagnosed with sciatica. The doctor told her to stay off her feet as much as possible and prescribed physical therapy.

Robin found this situation unbearable. She could not work and she could not even stand on her feet for more that five minutes before the pain made her sit down. She saw a physical therapist, who taught Robin some good stretching exercises and told her that stress was a contributing factor to her pain because her muscles were so tight, and she needed to do something to relieve them.

A friend of Robin's was taking yoga classes and suggested she practice it. Since Robin was in such a high-stress job, her friend thought yoga would do wonders for her. Robin decided to give it a try. After three months, she felt like a new woman. Robin experienced a real sense of peace and renewed energy after each session and the sciatica pain was completely gone. A career that she loved so much was saved, and she felt she had a new lease on life by practicing yoga.

Yoga may be the oldest form of exercise and relaxation. Its origins stem from Hinduism. It dates back as far as 3,000 B.C., to the Indus River Valley, where stones were found with pictures depicting humans engaging in the practice. It is derived from the Sanskrit word *yug* or *yuj* meaning union or join together. When you practice Yoga, you are joining your mind and body together in a union. Any person who practices it is known as a *yogi*, although the correct term for a male is *yogi*, and for a female it is *yogini*. It is similar to Tai Chi and ChiGong in that it is based on the principle of a universal life force or vital energy known as *prana* in India, as opposed to *chi* in China. According to *Yoga Journal* magazine, approximately 6 million people practice Yoga in the United States.

Many people think of yoga as a form of exercise where people bend themselves into contortions like a human pretzel. They think of it as exercises that cause pain and strain. Quite the opposite is true. It is never done with a force that will injure you. You perform the regimen in concert with your body's own specific capabilities. You do not have to be in perfect shape to start it. Yoga is a slow and gentle exercise if you wish. It can be more vigorous if you want to take it up a notch. It combines precise poses (known as *asanas*) and postures, with proper breathing, and meditation. Yoga is designed to create greater flexibility, strengthen muscles, and increase energy and overall wellness. It enables you to live a healthier and more fulfilling life.

Yoga is not a religion or cult, but a practice of techniques. It does not advocate any religious dogma or doctrine, or require a specific lifestyle such as being a monk. There is no dress code; comfortable clothing will do the trick.

The Benefits of Yoga

There are many distinct, yet related, schools or branches of Yoga, known as paths. In the West, Hatha Yoga has become the most popular path. It is a path of health with its accent on exercise, stretches, and positions to gain calm, peace, and tranquility, as well as physical well-being. Other paths focus on such areas as spirituality, wisdom, love, and serving others. All paths have the same goal or objective: to lead to a state of enlightenment.

Hatha Yoga's benefits are immediate and long-lasting. You relax the body with exercises, which in turn empties and quiets the mind. You add proper breathing and focus to it, and you control the mind, gaining inner peace and harmony. It is holistic in that it brings together the mind, body, and spirit.

The reasons for practicing yoga are many and varied. Since you are reading this book to get a grip on stress, consider yoga, as it will definitely destress and reenergize you. The series of yoga postures enable you to stretch and strengthen muscles. Your newfound flexibility will serve as an aid in preventing injuries, especially as you get older. Yoga is wonderful for the posture and enables you to walk more erect. Yoga helps in loosening the back muscles, preventing back spasms and pain.

Most of us breathe by taking shallow breaths, not using our full lung capacity. Yoga teaches you different methods of deeper, slower, conscious breathing, so that you take in more air. This helps the muscle cells get more oxygen so they can function better. The deep breathing also calms the mind. Focusing on the breath helps you to get in touch with how your body feels, both physically and mentally. It also enables the prana or energy to enter the body. Your senses become enhanced as you gain a keener awareness of your surroundings. Practice it and you will feel more vital and alive.

Make a Decision

In this chapter, I have given you five additional and different forms of exercise that all deliver stress relief. They all have similar benefits, with each having its own particular methodology of getting the job done. They all take a holistic approach to fitness. Look at them in terms of how much time you have, and how much stress you have. Think about which ones can be done at work to get on-the-spot relief. Consider your overall health and how you need to improve it. Determine which exercises are the most enjoyable, and which ones you can make a long-term commitment to doing, if any. The important thing is that you make a commitment to doing something to get a grip on stress.

6

WHAT'S FOOD
GOT TO DO WITH IT?

We all have those days at work when crises are mount-
ing, everything is going wrong, and we want to escape to some Caribbean island, lay on the beach, drink a
frozen Pina Colada, and just veg out. Instead, we go to the
vending machine and pop a few coins in for a candy bar or
bag of chips. We eat it because we are having such a rotten
day that we deserve every bite. The satisfaction lasts for two
minutes if we are lucky. The stress is still there, but we have
just put some more useless calories into our bodies. We want
something to make us feel better. We know we should not
do it, but we crave something. Why?

STRESS AND THE BRAIN CONNECTION

It would be wonderful if we could decide not to eat in response to stress. But there is more going on here than we realize. Part of this response lies in our brain chemistry.
Serotonin is a chemical substance that carries impulses to
nerve cells in the brain. When our brain cells need more
serotonin, as they do when we are under stress, they trigger
a craving for carbohydrate-rich foods because these foods

stimulate serotonin production. Food can act as a pain reliever and a tranquilizer. Stressors can deplete some of the nutrients we need to manage the stress response in our bodies, so it is important to eat the kinds of foods that will actually benefit our bodies, and help with our physical and physiological responses to stress.

Researchers at the James A. Haley Veterans Administration Medical Center, the University of South Florida, and Arizona State University found that chronically stressed rats who ate a high fat beef and excessive carbohydrate diet lost the ability to learn and retain new information. The reason was the combination of the high stress and the diet. When the rats were not stressed, but ate the same diet, they did not have a problem. Researcher David Diamond of the Tampa Veterans Administration Medical Center stated, "The implication is that the combination of a high fat diet and stress can interfere with the ability of the brain—in rats or people—to learn new information" (Conrad & Diamond, 2003). It is interesting that the correlation of diet and stress can be so highly connected in the brain.

Eating, Drinking, Smoking, and Stress

Eating, smoking, and drinking certain things can make us feel good for a short amount of time. Taking in caffeine by drinking coffee, tea, or soda to get us going and help us through the day actually stimulates the release of several stress hormones, and creates a hyperness that makes us more likely to interpret events as stressful. Eating a lot of sweets depletes the B vitamins in your system and can result in making you feel fatigued, anxious, and irritable. By having an excess of sugar in your body, blood glucose levels can fluctuate dramatically, which can cause headaches, tiredness, and moodiness, all symptoms that can compromise your ability to respond to stressful events. Chronic stress can make us use up more vitamins and minerals, and by using these up, it makes it harder to combat our reactions to stressful situations.

Many people will sooth the pain of a stressful day by going home and drinking a few beers or a few glasses of wine. The level of serotonin in the body increases with alcohol, and then after the alcohol is metabolized, the level decreases. We do feel better after a drink or two, but this decrease in serotonin is why we feel bad the morning after we have had one too many.

German researchers have shown that an abnormality in one of the genes associated with the body's stress response may predispose individuals to drink alcohol in response to stress (Sillaber, Rammes, Zimmermann, et al., 2002). The danger of making drinking a habit in response to stressful situations is just that; it can become a crutch that we cannot control.

According to the U.S. National Council on Alcoholism and Drug Dependence, if you are drinking heavily after a disappointment, a quarrel, or when the boss gives you a hard time, or if you have been drinking more heavily than usual when you have trouble or are under pressure, then these are warning signs of alcohol dependence. If you find yourself drinking more, or are afraid you might lose control, then stop drinking, and use that time to exercise or meditate instead. If this does not work, and you are having trouble stopping, then it is best to seek professional help.

Many people who smoke do so as a stress reliever. When a tense or unpleasant situation crops up they immediately crave a cigarette and light up as soon as they possibly can. After the first few inhalations, they start to feel a sense of calm. Are they really relieving their stress, or just setting their bodies up for cancer in the future? Andy C. Parrott of the University of East London, states,

> Regular smokers, therefore, experience periods of heightened stress between cigarettes, and smoking briefly restores their stress levels to normal. However, soon they need another cigarette to forestall abstinence symptoms from developing again. The repeated occurrence of negative moods between cigarettes means that smokers tend to experience slightly above-average levels of daily stress. Thus, nicotine dependency seems to be a direct cause of stress. Various surveys have shown that smokers report slightly higher levels of daily stress than do nonsmokers. (1999)

If you are a smoker, you may be contributing to your stress levels by doing the very thing you think is relieving your stress. By quitting smoking you can help to reduce your stress levels, and eliminate the health risks.

WHAT'S EATING YOU?

My friend, Dino, called me late one night. He had been in a car accident. Luckily, no one was injured, but his car was totaled. He asked me to pick him up and bring him home, which I was happy to do. Dino was shook up, and when he got home he immediately went to the refrigerator. Unfortunately, he found nothing to eat there, so he opened his cupboard and found a lone can of peas. I watched in shock and amazement as he opened the can and shoveled the cold peas into his mouth. He said the peas were better than nothing because he was absolutely famished, although he had a big dinner earlier that evening. Is Dino just an indiscriminate eater, or was there something else going on? I had many meals with Dino and knew he had better taste than that! Because of the accident, his system was in the fight-or-flight mode discussed earlier. The stress response revved him up, and his body was demanding more fuel making him feel ravished.

If you are feeling hungry when you should not be, the real culprit could be stress. This is especially true when you are chronically stressed. You end up with a constant urge to eat. If you often crave carbohydrates or foods with high sugar, crave food late at night, or eat to calm down when you are upset, then you are likely to be a stress eater. You may also be a stress eater if you:

- Eat when you have a crisis going on in your life.
- Feel eating helps you to cope with problems and situations.
- Eat when you feel things are just too much to handle.
- Are feeling uncomfortable at a social gathering or party, are feeling anxious and/or out of place, and snack on the food to "have something to do."
- Eat when you are not hungry.

Eating the Right Foods

Just the action of eating for some people produces a comforting feeling when they are under stress or when they are feeling down, lonely, or bored. The secret to combating obsessive, or stress-related eating is to eat the right foods at the right time. Doing this in tandem with exercising will ensure you get a grip on stress. If you are eating the right foods, you will not have those destructive cravings for unhealthy and useless calories.

By eating properly, you will have more energy and lose weight, as well as be able to handle stress more effectively.

You will be giving your body the correct balance of nutrients to reduce your stress levels and those cravings for junk food. Eating complex carbohydrates triggers your pancreas to secret insulin. This insulin allows the amino acid tryptophan to synthesize serotonin, and the increased serotonin will make you feel better and less stressed. Some foods high in tryptophan are: turkey, chicken, plain yogurt, almonds, cashews, and sunflower seeds.

Other foods can decrease the level of serotonin in your system. If your diet is high in protein, it will lower the level. Diets that are based on high protein are not good for people who are under constant stress or have high-stress jobs. The lowered serotonin levels only make it harder for them to cope. One of the reasons football players and boxers eat a high protein diet is that it makes them aggressive and ready to fight. The high level of serotonin coursing through their bodies causes them to be aggressive competitors.

Carbohydrate-rich foods produce more of that good feeling serotonin. That is why pizza, pasta, and macaroni and cheese are so appealing when we are stressed or anxious. But these same foods can put the weight on us, and soon we are wearing what we have eaten in a very unappealing way. But, not all carbohydrates are bad. Foods with complex carbohydrates are good for us. Complex carbs take longer to digest, give you energy that is long lasting, and contain lots of vitamins and minerals. Some foods with complex carbs are: sweet potatoes, squash, carrots, brown rice, whole wheat breads, whole grain cereals, beans, corn, and tomatoes.

Unrefined complex carbohydrates have high fiber, vitamins, and other nutrients. Foods like white bread and white rice are actually less filling and less nutritious because the carbohydrates have been refined. You can get that same comforting, less stressed feeling from eating unrefined complex carbohydrates, and gain more nutrition than you would by eating refined carbohydrates like white rice, pastas made with flour, potato chips, and pretzels. An added benefit is that unrefined complex carbs are less fattening. Foods that are low in fat and protein but high in complex carbohydrates can produce a calm and relaxing effect. Instead of snacking on a bag of chips when you are stressed, try eating some trail mix or granola. If the workplace is being hard on you, you need be good to yourself.

Foods with refined sugars have simple carbohydrates. Some foods with simple carbohydrates are: candy, cookies, cakes, soft drinks, and ice cream. These are all things we love to eat when we are stressed. One of the reasons for this is because these foods remind us of our childhood when we did not have to worry about health and calories. Because they are carbohydrates, they calm us. The problem is that refined sugars enter and leave the bloodstream so quickly that our energy does not last long and the sugars turn into fat.

Eating high fat foods like cheeses, meat, butter, rich sauces, sour cream, and mayonnaise, besides increasing your risk for heart attacks and strokes, make you feel tired and lethargic. The weight you gain will affect your health in a negative way, and you will not be happy with how you look, which turns into another stressor for you.

You can combat the effect of chronic stress weakening your immune system by eating fruits and vegetables. By doing this you gain valuable antioxidants. Beta-carotene is an antioxidant you can get by eating carrots, squash, and sweet potatoes. Citrus fruits provide vitamin C, another antioxidant that is great for combating stress. The weight you will lose just by switching from those high-calorie pizzas, burgers, and fries to high antioxidant vegetables and fruits is another reason to do it.

Timing Is Everything

Just as important as what you eat, is when you eat. If you are skipping breakfast and just having a cup of coffee in the morning, you are robbing your body of valuable energy and nutrients to face the stressors of the day. It is like a soldier going into battle without a weapon. A breakfast laden with fat and carbohydrates will make you sluggish and prevent you from functioning at your peak. Skipping meals and then eating fattening snacks is the worst thing you can do. Your body is storing those fattening snacks because it is not sure when you are going to eat again.

If you do not have time to eat, drink a fruit smoothie or eat a piece of fruit and drink a glass of juice. Sometimes, when I am in a hurry, I will eat a cup of whole grain cereal at work, without milk. It becomes like a snack and only takes a minute or two. As tempting as it is, do not reach for that glazed donut on the break room table at work. You will only be giving your body a quick sugar rush, empty calories, and more fat to feel guilty about.

Skipping meals can be easy when you just do not have the time to eat. Skipping breakfast, snacking on the wrong foods instead of eating lunch, then eating a big dinner and going to sleep on a full stomach is a sure-fire way to ensure health problems of all kinds in the future. Eating small meals, five to six times a day, will help your body and mind function at their peak. It is a great formula for weight loss because if you are not hungry, your body will not be storing food for energy, as it does with erratic eating patterns.

Take some fruit to work as a mid-morning snack, some nuts (go easy on the quantity as they are high in fat and calories), and vegetables like carrots and celery sticks for an afternoon snack. Eat small lunches with nutritious foods like skinless chicken breasts and fish without rich, fatty sauces, and salads without heavy, fattening dressings. Do not eat bread or pasta (unless it is whole wheat), cheeseburgers, or pizza. These foods will make it harder to handle stress, and you will go back to work feeling lethargic.

Keep your dinner meal portions moderate. Eat more vegetables and salads instead of starches. I always tell my audiences to remember: no white at night. This means eat little or no refined carbohydrates such as white bread, white rice, and noodles and pastas made with flour. Try eating fish, chicken, turkey, and lean pork for protein instead of a high fat steak that will lower your serotonin level. After dinner is a good time to walk off some stress and some of those calories. If you get hungry later in the evening have a light and healthy snack. Just make sure you are not going to sleep on a full stomach because it puts stress on your digestive system. Many people get heartburn, acid indigestion, and even bad dreams from doing this.

Keeping the Pleasure in Eating

Eating is one of life's greatest pleasures but you do not have to take the pleasure out of it to reduce stress and improve your health. You can have a healthy diet, lose weight, and still eat delicious and satisfying foods. There are many creative, low fat, low carb, low sugar cookbooks available these days. There are huge amounts of recipes on the Internet for healthy dishes. If you cannot cook, do not want to cook, or do not have the time, there are some healthy frozen entrees in the stores, although they tend to be high in sodium. Some supermarkets have precooked meals. Select the healthy ones and ask if they have been prepared with butter or oil, or contain high amounts of sugar. Go for the low fat, good carbs, low sugar meals. Try to keep creativity in your meals so that you do not get bored eating the same things over and over. This will only make you want to binge on things you should not. Give yourself a treat occasionally with a cup of ice cream or a piece of birthday cake at the office party. If you deny yourself too much, you will start to obsess about the foods you are missing, and this will make you want to give up eating healthy altogether.

When you eat out at restaurants you can still order healthy foods. Ask for chicken, turkey, or fish that is broiled without sauces. A good substitute for refined carbohydrates is to order more vegetables. Try a sweet potato instead of a mound of fat-laden mashed potatoes. Because so many people are on diets these days, most restaurants are happy to accommodate you. Stay away from junk foods and high fat, high carb, fast food meals. They are your worst enemy! Remember, if you are fueling your body with foods that are counterproductive to your health, you are only making it harder on yourself to combat the daily effects of stress. Try to make your healthy diet a way of life. Figure 6.1 shows you a small sampling of healthy restaurant food choices.

Remember to watch your portions. Do not eat until you are stuffed, but just until you feel comfortable. Restaurants tend to serve gargantuan portions, and many people feel they have to eat every bite. Maybe it is because we are paying for it that we feel it is a waste to leave it. If I am served a huge portion, I will eat just half of it and have the server box up the rest for me to take home. This eliminates the guilt of leaving it and the guilt of eating more than I should at one meal. When everyone at your table is ordering dessert, and you just cannot resist the siren song of that piece of chocolate pecan cheesecake, try taking just a bite or two from someone else's piece or splitting a piece with another person. Of course, you do not want to make a habit of this, but doing it once in a while will keep you from feeling deprived.

FIGURE 6.1   Restaurant Food Choices

Choose	*Instead of*
Pasta with marinara sauce (no meat).	Lasagna.
Grilled seafood.	Fried seafood.
Minestrone soup.	Cream of mushroom soup.
Veggie burgers.	Hamburgers.
Turkey sandwich on whole wheat bread.	Steak sandwich on a roll.
Barbequed chicken.	Beef or pork ribs.
Chicken fajitas.	Beef and/or cheese enchiladas.
Chicken taco.	Beef taco.
Broiled, grilled fish or chicken.	Fried chicken or fish.
Baked sweet potato with fat free sour cream.	Baked potato with "the works."
Steamed or grilled vegetable, no butter.	Vegetables with butter or sauces.
Herbal tea.	Coffee.

What Works Best

If you need to lose weight to get yourself back in good health, there are many diet plans you can go on. There seems to be a new diet plan popping up every week. The one thing you do not want to do is crash diet or take diet pills. These methods are hard on your system and it will make it more difficult for you to deal with stress. Besides, once you go off the diet or the pills, in time you will gain the weight back again. They are not a permanent solution for weight loss.

How do you know which plan is right for you? A diet that will stabilize blood sugars, consists of good carbohydrates and the complex carbs, along with protein that is low in fat and high in tryptophans (chicken, turkey), is the best combination to combat the effects of stress. A diet that requires

FIGURE 6.2 You Are What You Eat Quiz

Take the following quiz to determine whether your methods of coping with stress are healthy or unhealthy. Begin monitoring what you put into your body, and make changes accordingly.

	Yes	No
I strive to keep healthy by watching what I put in my body.	___	___
I do not smoke any type of tobacco or marijuana.	___	___
I limit my alcoholic drinks to one or two small drinks a day.	___	___
I do not take narcotic or illegal drugs.	___	___
I limit my caffeine from coffee, tea, sodas, and chocolate.	___	___
I drink at least six glasses of water per day.	___	___
I limit the amount of sugar I eat.	___	___
I limit the amount of fats I eat.	___	___
I limit the amount of carbohydrates I eat.	___	___
I limit junk food or fast food to once a week.	___	___
I take a multiple vitamin everyday.	___	___
I eat three meals a day, and do not skip breakfast.	___	___
I eat plenty of fiber, fruits, and vegetables.	___	___
I eat small to moderate portions of food.	___	___
I stop eating at least three hours before bedtime.	___	___

high protein and very little carbs is the exact opposite of what you need to control stress. You need a plan that will be easy to stick to and one that allows you the freedom to eat a variety of healthy foods. (See Figure 6.2.) Fad diets that require you to eat weird combinations of food like only hot dogs one day and only bananas the next may work in the short term to get rid of pounds, but you cannot stay on a diet like that forever. Besides, combinations like these do not give your body the fuel it needs to deal with stress. To combat stress and stay at a healthy weight, you need to make a commitment to eat healthy for the rest of your life.

7

TACKLING STRESS
WITH A TICKLE

Laughter is a powerful elixir of healthful benefits. The old adage that says, "laughter is the best medicine" rings true more than ever in a stress-filled world. Doctors have known for years that a patient who is laughing is going to recover quicker from sickness than someone who is angry and miserable. Laughter has a tremendous healing power. Humor helps us to destress because it is really difficult to feel anger, tension, and stress while you are laughing.

Laughter is usually caused by something humorous, but this is not always the case. Many people find themselves laughing at the little trials and tribulations that arise each day. Others are able to find laughter in absurd situations. It helps people to cope with personal and traumatic losses. Laughter brings us relief. It gives us strength to triumph over setbacks, and enables us to keep going, in spite of everyday roadblocks and obstacles.

THE BENEFITS OF LAUGHTER

There is no question that laughter reduces stress because it lowers some of the stress-creating hormones in our blood.

With hearty laughter, we are breathing faster and deeper—almost panting—and we take in more oxygen, cleansing the lungs. Our heartbeat speeds up, and we send more oxygen throughout our body. As a result, our muscles lose that tightness and tension discussed earlier. The facial jaw and throat muscles are stretched. The chest and stomach muscles are exercised. We do this over and over during prolonged laughter. After the laughter is over, the stomach muscles also deeply relax. It is almost like an aerobic workout, only without the sweat.

Laugh for the Health of It

Laughter has been linked to the amount of immunoglobin (IGA) found in our saliva. This substance is part of the body's natural immune system that fights off colds, the flu, and other respiratory problems. The more you laugh, the higher the level of IGA. It also enhances the level of the other natural killer known as T lymphocytes or T cells. People who laugh more have less stress and less sickness.

An old Jewish proverb states, "When you are hungry, sing; when you are hurt, laugh." Research has shown that laughter reduces pain. Laughter increases the amount of endorphins in our blood, which are powerful, natural painkillers. Author Norman Cousins recounted for us in his well-known bestseller, *Anatomy of an Illness* (1979), how he used humor and laughter to help cure himself of a painful connective tissue disease that threatened his life. He purposely left the hospital and spent hours reading humorous stories and watching humorous movies, such as the Marx Brothers, Candid Camera, and the Three Stooges. Amazingly, his pain subsided. He stated that 10 minutes of very hard laughter would result in about two hours of pain relief from his condition. He later concluded that the laughter was the main reason for changing the course of his illness.

Although the use of clowns at hospitals to help the healing process has not been researched and written about in medical journals extensively, there are many examples of this occurring. We all know the story of Dr. Patch Adams, who proved that clowns have the ability to get people to respond and make them laugh when they are very sick or depressed. Dr. Raymond Moody, a medical doctor, has written about numerous cases in his book, *Laugh After Laugh*. He states:

> In fact, had I not seen it with my own eyes and gathered many reports of it, I would be rather hesitant to mention it myself. It is that sometimes, through their antics, clowns can bring people back from severely withdrawn and unresponsive states even after all attempts by their doctors and nurses have failed. It is not at all unusual for clowns to be fully aware of this; everyone I know who has been a clown for a respectable period, and who makes it his practice to visit hospitals while dressed up and "in face" has his stories of this to tell. Doctors, as a group, are cognizant of it. (1978)

I have an old knee injury that flares up whenever I do certain activities. Over time, I have just learned to ignore it, and use positive self-talk and meditation (not medication) to decrease any pain. After a recent day of working in my yard, doing a lot of squatting, my knee was really irritated and painful. That evening, my wife and I went out with friends to the local comedy club to see a comedian. It was nonstop, hearty laughter for two hours. I realized halfway though his outrageous act that I no longer felt any pain or inflammation in the knee. A few hours after the show was over, the pain occasionally returned, but to a much lesser degree. Laughing was a great antidote for the pain.

Laughter has a tremendous positive impact on our emotional state. Comedian Milton Berle once said, "Laughter is an instant vacation." It stops us from thinking about the stress at work and the pressures of life. It enables us to detach ourselves from a situation, view it from a distance, and realize that it often is not as bad as we made it out to be. Humor reenergizes us.

Humor has been used as a coping tool for many people who have dealt with emotional turmoil in their childhood. I have seen interviews with comedian Richard Pryor discussing the fact that his mother was a prostitute, his father was violent, and he described his grandmother as mean and nasty. Pryor began to realize at an early age that he could make his family laugh. He quickly found out that if they were laughing at him, they would treat him much nicer. Humor helped him to cope with his emotional pain and suffering. Carol Burnett has described in interviews how she grew up in a family with alcoholic parents. She began to use humor to get her parents laughing, and keep them from arguing and yelling. It made her life easier, and allowed her to deal with the emotional upheavals. Humor and laughter allow us to conquer a painful past.

But it is not just comedians who use it to cope. I know many people who have learned to use humor to deal with the everyday stressors and absurdities that impact their lives. Learning to laugh in the face of tension and turmoil does wonders for us. Laughing at difficult situations enables us to disconnect ourselves from that situation, and look at it in a different light. Humor is like an escape chute that prevents you from flying into a rage or getting depressed. Humor helps you get a grip on an unpleasant situation, so you can see it through a new perspective.

Comedian Victor Borge said, "Laughter is the shortest distance between two people." Laughter connects us with other people when we are having social interaction. We laugh more when we are together with friends and relatives, than we do by ourselves. We laugh less with strangers, but a humorous comment can immediately help develop rapport and get people talking together. It helps us to create faster and long-lasting relationships. People want to be around others with whom they can laugh. People are attracted to, and want to spend time with funny people.

When I was a child, I learned the tremendous joy that laughter could bring to others. My family lived on the top floor of a two-story house, with my maternal grandparents living downstairs. I was always visiting with my grandparents, and at times it seemed as though I spent more time with them than my own parents. I really enjoyed their company, as they were both born in Southern Italy and had a real zest for life. My grandmother, Filomena DeAngelo, in particular had a tremendous sense of humor. She was the one who would start dancing the tarantella at family picnics, while my grandfather played some serious bocce, a game that Italian Americans are taking up again in great numbers. Grandma DeAngelo was always asking me to tell her jokes, perform a dance, or do anything I could think of that was funny. I always responded, bringing her lots of laughter and joy.

Of course I enjoyed the attention it brought me. I soon realized that I could make students at school laugh, and sometimes even my teachers. They would often send notes home or make comments on my report card that I should concentrate on my studies and stop trying to be the class clown. My father used to read these comments, and always asked me in a terse manner, "What do you think you are: a comedian?" I guess the answer was yes. What I gleaned from this success was the desire to be in front of people, speaking to them, and also making them laugh. I had a desire to tell funny stories to as many people as I could. Humor really helped me to find a niche in my life. But more than that, it enabled me to keep stress levels down when things were hectic and fast-paced. It also helped me to get through any tough times. Laughing at the absurdity of some things helps you to get through those times in life when we feel like we need to scream.

I use a lot of humor in my seminars, because it keeps people alert, they learn faster, and it makes it fun. Their mind is more open, as the laughter keeps the oxygen flowing. They are more tuned in, waiting for a funny comment or humorous anecdote. I notice that the smaller the group, the less laughter there is. I also notice, when the audience is a majority of women, the laughter is always louder. When the audience is a majority of men, the women always laugh first, and it sends a signal to the men it is all right to laugh. I often wonder if there is a connection between these events and the fact that women have less heart disease and live longer than men.

I believe that laughter increases your life span. Witness, for example, the many comedians who not only lived into their nineties and to 100 (Bob Hope, Milton Berle, and George Burns), but also worked up to a very old age. Many of them stated that making others laugh, and constantly laughing had kept their minds thriving and their bodies healthy. Research backs this up. "Studies of those who live into their nineties or a second century consistently show that high among the most common characteristics of elders is a healthy sense of humor" (Lizotte & Litwak, 1995). To put it mildly, there is no downside to humor. It does not cost anything and it can be contagious, creating positive benefits for others.

LETTING MORE LAUGHTER INTO YOUR LIFE

Not many people, except comedians and satirists, go throughout their day searching for humor and laughter. Try this for a
week. Make a conscious effort to hear or see something humorous as you go throughout your day. You are surrounded
by it, but do not realize it. Make a mark on a small piece of paper every time you laugh. If it is really hilarious, make a detailed note of it, because you must share it with others. You
want to make them laugh, which also makes you laugh more.
If you make a conscious effort to find the humor in everyday
life, you will probably have more marks on the paper as the
week goes on. This will get you in the habit of finding the
funny in things. I do this all the time, as I create humorous
anecdotes and stories for my seminars by observing humorous and absurd things that happen to myself and others.

Be on the Lookout

Many times humor is available for you to purchase. My wife
and I search out stores that carry items that make us laugh.
We visit stores that carry funny greeting cards, humorous
signs, and outrageous pillows and doormats. We try to send
only humorous cards for birthdays of friends and relatives.
Do not overlook secondhand shops as they can be a bo-
nanza for finding discarded humorous items.

There are many funny signs in public places. Over the
years I have taken pictures of some of them and have used
them in my seminars. People find them hysterical. One
sign that appears frequently in hotel room showers states,
"Please place shower curtain inside tub before turning on
water." Whenever I see it, I tell the audience what a difficult time I had taking all those shower curtain hooks off,

and how hard it was to shower while standing on the shower curtain.

One hotel in which I stayed had the most difficult shower apparatus for turning on the water, switching the water from bath to shower, and regulating the temperature. It worked like it was invented by a lunatic. It took me some time to figure out how it operated. I almost called the front desk to ask how it worked, but did not want to appear stupid. As I worked my way through the situation, I realized how absurd it was, and knew I must share it with the audience. I was presenting a keynote to about 1,500 people for a large association. I opened my speech with the question, "Was anybody else almost late today because they could not figure out how the shower worked, or was it just me?" The place roared with laughter and people applauded. Humor and absurdity surround us all the time. You must keep a keen eye out for it.

Put on a Happy Face

A smile connects you to other people. You are more apt to meet people at social events if you are laughing with others or smiling. I frequently have the opportunity to attend cocktail events of groups that I am speaking to the next day. I know no one in the group, and usually don't have a name tag yet. I have found that if I just stand around by myself and just put a slight smile on my face, people will usually just come up and begin talking.

I have mentioned in other chapters about the benefits of smiling, and how it can make you feel better. I have found that if I smile in tense or annoying situations, it seems to calm me down. Even if I fake the smile, it somehow has a tranquilizing effect. I use this when I am waiting in traffic, and everyone else is cursing at the other cars and red lights.

I use it when I am standing in a long line at a store when everyone else is whining and complaining about the waste of time. I figure if I am going to be sitting in traffic or stuck in a line, I might as well stay calm, feel good, and relax. Why make myself miserable? The choice is yours: Accept the wait and feel good afterwards or become emotional over it, and be angry and stressed out.

Brainstorm Fun Ideas

Have you ever reflected on what really makes you laugh or what type of sense of humor you have? Most people do not analyze what makes them laugh the hardest and longest. Do you like jokes, stories, improvisation, satire, or fun games? Whatever it is that tickles your funny bone, you need to actively do more of it. Very few people ever sit down and consciously create a list of fun things to do: the kinds of things that will get you laughing. Sure, humorous things happen by chance and make you laugh. But you will laugh much more if you actively seek out amusing activities to do alone and with family and friends. See Figure 7.1 for some ideas.

Hang Out with Funny, Positive People

I know this one sounds obvious, but we need to do more of it. Make a list of all your close friends, and rate them on a scale of one to five as to how much fun they are, or how much time you spend laughing with them. Are you having only serious conversations, or do you share a lot of humor? If it is all serious, that's fine, but you need to also develop positive friendships with fun, upbeat people. Their fun and laughter is contagious. I have found that the best friendships my wife and I have encompass loads of laughter, and sometimes downright silliness. My dear friend Bill, whom I

FIGURE 7.1   Looking for Laughs

Comedy clubs.
Comedy channel.
Funny sitcoms.
Card shops.
Joke books.
Funny movies (old and new).
Stand-up comedy performances on tape, CD, and DVD.
Fun games.
Humorous stories (yours and others).
Clip and collect or post cartoons.
Stores with funny cards, pillows, doormats, signs, and slogans.
Magic shops.
Second-hand stores.
Toy store and hobby shops.
Pet stores and zoos.
Watching kids play.

met in college as a roommate, has got the wackiest sense of humor. He is downright silly, but a true joy to be around. He never lost the sense of humor he had in college. I often tell him he is still a sophomore. We never stop laughing when we chat by phone or when we are together. It is something that has bonded us for life.

My wonderful friend Gary, who is like a brother to me, has the most upbeat, positive attitude about everything in life. He truly filters it all through rose color glasses. He is always laughing and cheerful. He also has a childlike curiosity, embracing all that is new. His wife, Alice, has the most wonderful, warm glowing smile. People are drawn to them. It is quite fascinating to watch how they both can work a room with those magnetic personalities.

Learn to Laugh at Yourself

We all do goofy, silly things that make us look foolish. We all make embarrassing mistakes. We must learn to see the humor in them and laugh at ourselves. Telling embarrassing stories can be a fun event at social gatherings. I have asked people to share these stories on numerous occasions, and the stories people tell are hilarious. You make others laugh, and you realize that others are human just like you.

I often tell the story about when I was a senior in college, and my roommate Bill and I were invited to another student's house for a weekend. The following morning, when we all sat down for breakfast with the other student's family, his mother brought over a large platter of bacon and eggs to the table and handed it to me. The plates had not been set yet, just the silverware, so I assumed that she was serving me my meal first. I thought that it was a big portion, but I was really hungry and knew I could handle it. I put the platter down, and started eating from it. You cannot imagine the embarrassment and even humiliation I felt when everyone started laughing and teasing me because the platter was for everyone, not just me. I was teased for many years about this, and Bill still brings it up in front of groups of people. I guess I learned to never assume anything ever again. You must learn to laugh at yourself, which I do all the time.

Look for the Humor in Your Misfortune

This is a feat that many feel is difficult to accomplish. But we all have misfortune, and we all have losses that bring pain. We all fail at times. If you put your mind, heart, and soul into searching through most of your misfortunate events, you can always find something humorous, or even a silver lining. But, you must change your mind-set. You have to think positive thoughts, and really hunt for the good aspect of situations and events that happen to you. You have to search for the humor and irony in the event.

At this point you might be thinking, "That's easy for you to say." It is, but I like everyone else have had my share of difficult situations and setbacks. Keeping an upbeat attitude and sense of humor helped get me through all of them. I always learned to look for the good that came from it, and what I learned from it. My greatest mistakes and biggest failures turned out to be, in many ways, the setbacks that propelled me ahead to a new goal or accomplishment. When I look back in retrospect at misfortune, I always find something to chuckle about.

Share Fun and Laughs with Friends

Having a good time with friends and sharing laughter is one of the best ways to destress. Some of the greatest times my wife and I have had are at social events with friends, enjoying things like dinner parties, wine tastings at each other's homes, or going out together. Our good friend Donna, who is a party maven, has luncheons for all her female friends several times a year. Donna is a creative lady and she plans each luncheon with a theme. One was a jewelry exchange where guests bought and sold their unwanted jewelry to each other. At another, she planned a day at the spa in her home. She hired a masseur, and the guests had massages, facials, manicures, and other relaxing and pleasant experiences to go along with the luncheon. The best party she ever gave was for couples, and everyone brought jokes, funny poems, or funny stories to share. It was a side-splitting night, and one that we laugh about to this day.

EMPLOYEES JUST WANT TO HAVE FUN

Since we are all under tremendous pressure to be more productive with less support, it makes sense that we should have some time to have fun and be silly. Having fun in the workplace has a positive effect on an entire organization. Herb Kelleher, founder of Southwest Airlines, stated, "There is no reason that work has to be suffused with seriousness. Professionalism can be worn lightly. Fun is a stimulant. They enjoy their work and are more productive." Humor at work has a tremendous impact on relieving the boredom of rote and repetitive jobs. It lowers fatigue and stress, and prevents burnout. Fun makes employees more creative and productive, and it reduces costly errors. Employees who laugh are less likely to be late or absent. They are more satisfied with their work, and the work becomes more meaningful. They are less likely to leave. When they are happy, they make customers happy. As a result, fun in the workplace improves the bottom line.

Some might think that having fun at work might be a time waster and go against the methods of time management I discuss in Chapter 8. Actually, quite the opposite is true. Humor and laughter clear the mind and enable the brain to function better. Fun relaxes and recharges people. When people are laughing, they treat each other better, and with greater courtesy. Not only is the laughter contagious, but so is the courtesy, and this can only lead to greater productivity.

Some organizations have begun using humor consultants to teach people how to have good, clean, healthy fun. These consultants are hired to implement programs to boost morale, creativity, and job satisfaction. There is research to support that this works. According to Dr. William Fry of Stanford Medical School, laughter boosts cardiovascular fitness by lowering blood pressure and heart rate. It also reduces pain perception, stimulates blood flow, strengthens the immune system, and reduces the levels of hormones that create stress, all of which have positive effects on the person's creativity and productivity. (Swift & Swift, 1994)

Here is a sampling of some fun guidelines and suggestions. Most of them have come from suggestions of my seminar participants who have boasted of these ideas. What is appropriate at your workplace will be different from others. See how you can adapt these ideas to fit your culture.

The Leader Sets the Pace

There is an old expression in the Yukon that says, "The speed of the leader is the speed of the pack." The leader sets the tone and the pace. If you are the leader of your organization or department, you must lead by example. If you never have fun or smile, and are known to frown upon fun, your employees will be afraid to have fun. If you lighten up, they will lighten up. When you laugh, they will know it is okay to laugh. When you show that you are more human and like to keep it light, it will help relieve employees of any tension and stress. You will connect better with your people.

Take the time to seriously reflect on the systems, policies, and procedures you have in place. Do they contain obstacles or barriers to having fun? What needs to be changed? Sometimes just making small changes can make a gigantic difference. If you are not sure, start asking your people this question: What obstacles prevent us from having fun around here? Then listen carefully, but more importantly, implement some of their ideas.

Set Parameters

Once you have made the commitment to lighten up, it is best to create some parameters. Most people do not need to be told what constitutes good-natured fun. However, some people always want to push the envelope, and you could have some legal ramifications. Set some rules and guidelines, letting people know that the following are not tolerated: practical jokes and pranks, harassment, sexual jokes or comments, ethnic comments, negative or sarcastic comments about people or the organization, and anything else deemed offensive. If there are people who do not want to be part of creating or having fun (and there will be), do not make it mandatory.

Get People Involved

If you are not in a leadership position, you can certainly get involved and make suggestions to those who are. It is easy to create a laugh committee with a fun czar being the leader. Ask people what having fun on the job means. Have them brainstorm fun ideas that can occur during work hours, and fun events to build team spirit and morale after work. Rotate the members of the committee and the czar every few months, so you keep bringing in fresh ideas. Put up a silly suggestion box so others can suggest fun ideas to the committee. To keep the flow of suggestions coming in, have the committee respond to the suggestions within two days.

Yuk Yuk Bulletin Board

I believe that a bulletin board that creates fun, makes people laugh, and boosts morale is an absolute necessity. This is so inexpensive and you get so many positive returns from it. Have people bring in cartoons, jokes, and funny or ironic stories. Broadcast positive news about employees' personal lives. If they accomplished anything special in their personal or work lives, such as getting a degree or certification, post it. If they had a special event such as birthday, anniversary, or birth in the family, let everyone know. People love to have others ask them about something they accomplished, and brag about themselves. Paper the wall with humorous greeting cards. People will laugh about them for days. They look forward to seeing new cards and exciting bits of news.

Theme Days

Have a theme day where everybody wears clothes with a common theme such as a Western day. Try an ethnic food day, where everyone brings in food from a specific country, such as Italy, China, or France to share at lunch. Or, ask everyone to bring in a baby picture and have a contest to match the picture to the adult. Have a company office party built around a specific idea or theme. Just to be crazy, have people wear mix and match clothing that does not go together. Why save costumes and dressing silly only for Halloween? Try an ugly outfit day, or ugly hat day.

Silly Job Titles

Some seminar participants have told me they create silly job titles for every position. They actually have contests to see who can come up with the most creative or outlandish titles for different positions. They give great, fun prizes to the winner.

Add Humor to Meetings

In a later chapter, I discuss how to run shorter and more efficient meetings. You can also add humor to those meetings, especially if the topics are serious. Don't be afraid to start meetings with a cartoon, joke, or funny story. I know some firms that have made a meeting room into a fun room with a basketball hoop or a putting green. In some cases, people bring in funny toys and games. I have seen some organizations share stories in a lighthearted manner at meetings about the most absurd things that happened, or silly mistakes that people make. Not only does it get people laughing, but it makes everyone realize that others make mistakes also. It can also serve as a valuable learning tool, so the mistakes are not repeated.

One method that I have facilitated that has gotten lots of laughs and greatly relieved stress is what I call the "The Absurd Add On Story." At a meeting, someone brings up a mistake or error they experienced, and makes up some absurd negative consequence of the event, that is well beyond the truth. The story goes around from person to person, each taking a chance at adding an even more absurd consequence to it. I have seen this work as an amazing pressure release. Everyone realizes that everyone makes mistakes and they often do not turn out as bad as they seem. After that, a brainstorming session follows on how to correct the mistake so it never reoccurs. It may seem this goes against the principles of sound time management, but anything that is a positive learning experience, prevents future mistakes, creates fun, and relieves stress is well worth the time. And speaking of time, in Chapter 9, we will explore how you can better manage your time, and in turn better manage your stress.

8

STAYING SANE
WHILE TRAVELING
AT WARPED SPEED

The 1960s ushered in a cultural revolution, and started our society traveling at the warped speed it moves at today. By the mid-1960s, women were no longer content to be "just homemakers," and wanted to achieve and have more in life. This was the beginning of how our society would become what it is now: people living their lives at an insane pace. No longer do we have clear cut roles in life, as we did prior to the 1960s. Back then, husbands had careers, wives were the homemakers and caretakers of the children, and if necessary, their elderly parents.

As ideal as this may sound to some, it was not. Most women felt very empty. Some women wanted to blaze their own trails, some just wanted to be able to have a better life, and some just wanted to be able to provide for their families. Our society has changed in dramatic ways. Today, our roles in life are many, and the clear cut distinctions that existed back then are gone. Men are doing the grocery shopping, preparing meals, taking care of the children, doing laundry, and other chores that used to be a woman's domain. Many people are single parents who are doing it all. With all of today's time-saving devices, we now have less free time than we did back in the 1960s. No wonder we are feeling so over-whelmed!

The days of putting in a 40-hour work week are a thing of the past. With all the downsizing and layoffs that have taken place, the amount of work has not downsized. People are working harder and longer hours. Some are working more to increase their chances of promotion, or to escape their personal problems or unhappy home lives. Whatever the reasons, work takes up large chunks of time that used to be devoted to family, friends, hobbies, or ourselves.

Technology has infiltrated our lives making it harder to escape work even when we are golfing, exercising, or just enjoying a tranquil moment looking at a beautiful sunset. It seems that the demands of work are constantly lurking in the background, nagging at us even when we are trying to escape from them. We tell ourselves it will only take a minute to answer that email, or retrieve that voicemail on the cell phone. Instead, those few minutes so often turn into an hour. Before we know it, precious time has been insidi-ously eaten away; time that could have been spent with spouses, children, parents, or others that are important in our lives.

TRYING TO BALANCE IT ALL

In a 2001 survey conducted by the Radcliffe Public Policy Center, 82 percent of men and 85 percent of women, ages 20 to 39, placed family time at the top of their work/life priori-ties. In a 2001 study by Rutgers University, and the Univer-sity of Connecticut, 90 percent of working adults said they are concerned that they do not spend enough time with their families. A work/life balance survey conducted in 2002 by

TrueCareers found that 70 percent of more than 1,500 respondents said they do not have a healthy balance between their personal and work lives (Lockwood, 2003). Everyone wants a balanced life, but it is as elusive as winning the lottery. We keep trying for it, but it does not happen. Many of us cannot stop thinking about work in our off hours. This robs us of the mental relaxation time that helps us to de-stress, and robs our loved ones of having us in the present moment with them, which is where we need to be.

The Have to Do's

So much of our free time is spent on the have to do's. After work, we have to pick the kids up from school, have to face a mountain of laundry that has to be done so everyone has clean clothes for the next day, have to prepare dinner, and have to do the dinner dishes. Then we have to help the kids with their homework, have to take out the trash, have to go through the stack of mail, have to pay the bills, have to check our emails, and on and on. Each day is a relentless list of have to do's, and if we do not do these things the stress and guilt kick in. We cannot help asking ourselves, "Is this what life is all about?"

Is That All There Is?

Life, like a diamond, is many faceted, precious, hard, and beautiful all at the same time. It sparkles constantly and people get a sense of joy from it. But, we all have times when our lives lose their sparkle and joy, and life seems just downright hard. All we seem to have are responsibilities and demands, and we know something is missing. We feel disconnected from life in some way, and we ask ourselves, "Is that all there is?" The purpose of life is to live it as fulfilled as we can, to try to reach our maximum potential, and to experience all that life has to offer. We cannot do that if we are living life with our nose to the grindstone all the time. In order to feel happy, we have to have the sparkle. Take the quiz in Figure 8.1 to see if you have that sparkle.

If you answered yes to any one of these questions, then you have to reexamine the way you are living your life. You only get one chance at it, and you are responsible for making it the best it can be. Yes, life is hard, it can be tedious, and at times downright miserable. But, it should not be this way constantly. You do not have control over all the factors in your life, but you can control how you live it. Life is meant to be enjoyed, and experiencing pleasure, joy, and happiness are wonderful antidotes for relieving stress.

Lack of Balance

A lack of balance in people's lives can lead to disastrous consequences. It fuels stress and job burnout, and it can even contribute to diseases and premature death. Many divorces have been caused by a lack of balance because spouses and

FIGURE 8.1   Life Luster Quiz

Do you feel	Yes	No
That your life is out of whack?	____	____
That something is missing?	____	____
That your life is dull and boring?	____	____
That your life is a constant juggling act and you are a bad juggler?	____	____
That your life is too routine and repetitive?	____	____
That you want to run away from it all?	____	____
That your life has lost its sparkle?	____	____

families have been relegated to second or third place. A lack of balance drains our energy and enthusiasm for life. With the constant juggling of all the responsibilities that is required in our daily lives, it is very easy to drop a few of them, and forget to pick them up. But, so many of us drop the most important responsibilities—our families, friends, and ourselves—for demands, that in the future, will not make a bit of difference in our lives or the lives of our loved ones. Keeping our lives in balance is something that has to be consciously worked at. Like a captain of a ship, we have to be aware of our course and navigate it through the rough and rocky spots. If we just drift along, with no direction, we will become lost in a sea of regrets.

Think about the percent of time you spend during the week on each of the following:

Working.   _____%
Family.   _____%
Friends.   _____%
Fun and entertainment.   _____%
Exercise and physical activities.   _____%
Spiritual/religious pursuits.   _____%

Does it look like your life is out of balance?

Are You a Slaveaholic?

The biggest portions of our lives are spent working. Working can give us a sense of fulfillment and a sense of self. Working gives us the resources to provide for ourselves and our families. We have to work to live. But, ask yourself, are you working to live or living to work? If you are putting in long days working, stop and think about why you are working so much. Take the test in Figure 8.2.

FIGURE 8.2 Slaveaholic Test

	Yes	No
I am overcome by guilt when I am not working.	___	___
I am constantly thinking about work when I am not working.	___	___
Vacations are of no interest to me.	___	___
I call or email my office several times a day when on vacation.	___	___
I feel that leisure time should be spent doing important work.	___	___
I work in bed before getting ready to go to sleep.	___	___
I hardly ever spend time with my family and friends.	___	___
My closest friends are my accountant, lawyer, and other co-workers.	___	___
All my goals in life are related to my career or job.	___	___
I only feel satisfied and content when I am working.	___	___

If you can answer yes to just a few of the quiz questions, then you are a slaveaholic. If work has taken over so many aspects of your life, then you are a slave to working. Of course, there are times when we are required to do more on the job, but when this becomes the norm and you are so wrapped up in it, you must take a good hard look at your reasons. Is what you are doing really so important that you have to miss out on your child's school play, or not be available on weekends to your family? There is no way to recover those precious times you missed.

What are the real reasons you are so wrapped up in work? Many people use work as an escape. If they have personal problems, work can keep them from dealing with them. If they are unhappy about their home life, work becomes a great escape. So often that great escape can lead to divorce or disintegration of the family. Many times, we are working to escape ourselves. By working so much, it keeps us from thinking about aspects of ourselves with which we cannot cope. Working can easily become a panacea for dealing with the negative parts of ourselves or our lives so that we are essentially living to work.

Is the Wanting Worth It?

We live in the best and yet worst of times. There are more material goods to choose from than at any other time in our country's history. We are constantly being enticed with newer technology, bigger houses, bigger TV's, nicer cars, designer clothes, plastic surgery, and everything the media tells us we need to make our lives happier. All this consumerism, which may be good for the economy, has made consumer junkies out of a lot of people. I call it the disease of "have to have it." Too many of us are infected with it, and are slaving away at work in order to be able to get the next fix of whatever it is that we cannot live without. We are only able to see the short-term pleasures of having the best of the best, and rarely, if ever, look at the toll it takes on the quality of the lives we lead or the lives our children are leading. Some people find meaning in their lives by purchasing the next acquisition they have to have. Too often material desires are so strong that our values become distorted. If you see yourself in this picture, ask yourself:

- What am I missing in life by putting in so many extra hours at work to be able to buy everything I want?
- Is it so important that I need to sacrifice time I could spend with my loved ones?
- Will I lose relationships and closeness with people that are important to me because I want to have so many material things?

In other words, is the wanting worth it? Your children will not be happier that they have a brand new SUV to ride around in than they would if you were home earlier to talk to them about a problem they have.

My friend, Jeff, was so caught up in this addiction, that he spent very little time at home. One night, he received an email at work. It was from his eight-year-old son, and he was begging him to quit working so that he could see him more. It was the wake-up call that Jeff needed in order to put his priorities back into perspective.

If you are having trouble tearing yourself away from work, think about this: How long would it take for you to be replaced at work before the company would be back to normal? Now, think about how long the people in your life would miss you if you no longer existed. Who would be impacted more by the loss of you—your place of work or your family and friends?

The Value of a Balanced Life

Having your life in sync will greatly reduce the stress of worrying about everything that you are not doing or should be doing. The drain on your energy and enthusiasm from feeling anxious, guilty, and overwhelmed will be much less. If you are married, you will have a better chance of staying married than if your life is out of balance.

At work, you will not be as prone to feeling burned out. You will find that you can manage your time more efficiently. If you manage people, you will be able to do your job better, and will relate to your employees better. Communications with co-workers will get better as well because you can focus on what is important and what is not. Everything is put into perspective.

IF YOU DO NOT KNOW WHERE YOU
ARE GOING, ANY ROAD WILL TAKE YOU THERE

What can you do to eliminate the stress and pressure of trying to live a balanced, well-rounded life? Start by looking inward and do some traveling in time. Picture yourself at the end of your life. What do you want your life to have been about? Make a list of the achievements you want to have accomplished by that time. Who are the people that enriched your life? Whose lives have you have enriched during your time on earth? Has your living made a difference, and to whom? Why? This will give you a bigger picture of what living is really supposed to be about.

Once you figure out what you want your life to be about, create a personal mission statement. This works well for businesses, but it will also help you keep on track. Knowing what your mission in life is gives you a purpose and direction. For example, a mission statement might be: "I will be there for my family and friends, physically, emotionally, spiritually, and lovingly. I will take care of myself, give myself what I need to be happy, and strive to be a better person every day." It can be long or short as long as it encompasses what you want your life to be about. This will help to bring balance to your life. The most valuable gift we have is life itself, and so many of us live it with no direction, no purpose, and no meaning. This is not a dress rehearsal, this is the real thing, and we only get one try at it.

Once you have your mission statement, write it down in several places (e.g., a sticky note placed on your bathroom mirror and your computer at work). Put it on your PDA, or in your daily planner. Make sure it is where you can see it frequently and be reminded of it often. This will keep you on the path you have chosen for yourself. List the obstacles that get in your way and try to find ways around them. This requires some time and effort, but it will be well worth it if you make the changes you need to balance and direct your life. Brainstorm for ways to get around the roadblocks that stand in your path.

Set Your Priorities

Let's go back to the percentage list you filled out previously showing how your life looks at present. Now, fill in the percentage of time you should be devoting to each of the following areas listed so that you can balance each aspect of your life. Do not be concerned about how you are going to accomplish these percentages at this point.

Working.	_____%
Family.	_____%
Friends.	_____%
Fun and entertainment.	_____%
Exercise and physical activities.	_____%
Spiritual/religious pursuits.	_____%

Keep these percentages in mind as we discuss how to achieve them.

Make a Commitment

Keeping balance in your life takes a real commitment, and it is something that has to be worked at constantly. Commit to achieving this goal, and keep your personal mission statement foremost in your mind for directing you to achieve your daily efforts.

Keep Track of Personal Time

To better determine how you are spending your personal time, try keeping track of it with a daily log for two weeks. This will give you a better picture of where and how you are spending your time off of work. It might surprise you to find that you have quality time that is being wasted, or that you need to rearrange things and do certain things at different times in order to free you up for more leisure time.

Be Creative and Flexible

The key to making more time with your loved ones is to plan and schedule in the time just as you would a meeting with employees. Think about how you can squeeze in time to meet. Be creative. If you and your family cannot make time to have dinner together because Britney has a dance class, Dylan has a basketball game, and your husband does not come home until 7:30 at night, then plan on the family meeting at 9:00 P.M. You can go over homework, talk about each other's day, and discuss problems, disappointments, or just have fun together. Make it mandatory that everyone show up—no excuses! Schedule this as a regular event at least three times a week. Let everyone know how important it is and how it will strengthen family ties.

Do make an effort to have dinner together when you can. This does not mean that Dad or Mom calls on their cell phone at dinnertime to talk to the kids. It does not have the same effect as being there in the moment with them. Children need to know they are important to their parent or parents; that they have a top spot in their parent's busy life. They need to feel loved and wanted, and by not being there it sends a negative message to them: You are not that important. Cut off all business contacts while you are spending time with the family. Make loved ones know they are your top priority when you are with them and they have your undivided attention.

Talk with Each Other

There will be times, of course, when work or other obligations have to come first. We all know that having a balanced life is not like walking down a straight path; there will be ruts and curves along the way. Some situations are unavoidable, like when you have to attend a business meeting out of town, and your anniversary is on the same day you are gone. Good lines of communication are vital between you and your loved ones. Everyone needs to be able to express their feelings open and honestly.

Understanding and flexibility are keys to managing these roadblocks. You need to know if your family is feeling neglected or resentful so that you can work on making things better. If there are changes that need to be made, they have to be discussed and worked out so that no one feels neglected or unloved.

Let Them Know You Care

The best thing you can do for loved ones and friends is to let them know, every day, how much you value them. If you cannot be with them to express this, then call them, email them, or send them a fax. Just make sure they get the message of how important they are in your life. It will do wonders to build relationships, and it only takes a few minutes of your time—time that could not be better spent.

Outsourcing

If you can swing it financially, think of which chores and responsibilities can be done by paying someone else to do them. Housecleaning, lawn maintenance, home repairs, babysitting, preparing meals, and grocery shopping can all be outsourced. If you cannot afford it, think about exchanging chores with friends or relatives. Try babysitting a friend's children while they grocery shop for both of you so that you can tackle some home chores while watching all the kids. Get creative and brainstorm with other working friends and relatives and discover how each may have an expertise or time available that can be exchanged with one another. Start a support group with several people so each of you can rely on one another when you need to.

Make the Most of It

Standing in line at the bank, sitting in traffic, or waiting in a doctor's office are all frustrating and stressful experiences especially when our lives are so full and we cannot afford to waste even a minute. Reduce the stress and frustration by getting things accomplished like making a "to do" list, doing routine paperwork at the doctor's office, updating your daily planner, and reading work-related materials or educational materials. If you have a laptop computer, take it with you to work on while waiting at doctor appointments. While in the car, listen to motivational or humorous tapes that will boost your spirits and outlook. If you are achieving something during these times, it will relieve the stress of feeling like you are losing valuable moments. Good time management is crucial for putting your life in balance.

Just Say No

Some people feel that they have to do everything that is asked of them. Others simply cannot disappoint people, and because of this they are overwhelmed by too much to do. Examine the demands that are being put upon you by others at work and at home. If they are unreasonable or are interfering with your life balance do not be afraid to say no.

Unnecessary interruptions during the workday need to be eliminated. Sometimes people will interrupt you with a trivial "emergency" or with some task they do not want to handle, and dump it on you instead. Some employees just want to spend time socializing. You have to be able to draw the line and let people know that enough is enough. In Chapter 9 I will show you how to be a good manager of your time. One of the most important skills is having the ability to just say no.

Hang Up the Halo

- Do you find yourself constantly redoing a task or project because it's not quite right?
- Do you feel uncomfortable when people praise or compliment you on something you have done?
- Do you feel that you are critical of your own accomplishments most of the time?
- Do you feel you must do everything, so things will be done right?

These are classic symptoms of a perfectionist. People place unnecessary stress on themselves being consumed by this trait. If you feel you are a perfectionist, then hang up your halo! Do not get me wrong, there are times when perfectionism is a good thing. I would want my heart surgeon to be a perfectionist. I do not need my floors cleaned every day, though. Perfectionism is a matter of priorities. It is a hard habit to break, and most of this behavior is done unconsciously. If you stop to think about it when you are doing it and work at eliminating it, your life will ease up considerably. The extra time you waste on doing things that do not have to be done perfectly can be spent doing something relaxing and stress-free. If you are preparing dinner for guests and it does not come out perfectly, as a perfectionist, you will most likely get all stressed out over it, and not enjoy the evening as much as you should. The important thing is that you are spending time having fun with friends, not that the meal was not quite up to par.

Family Fun

Playing together as a family is one of the best things you can do to strengthen family bonds. Even if you can only spare an hour or two to do something fun together, the effect will be long lasting for the family. Play a game of hoops, go to the movies, the zoo, hiking, or to a park together as often as you can. Taking family vacations and long weekends to a new destination that can be experienced together will renew everyone's spirit and closeness.

Love and Sex

A 2001 survey that appeared on AARP's web site entitled, "Having Fun as We Age: A Survey of Adult Fun Styles," found that only 37 percent of men and 34 percent of women find the time to engage in making love. Making love is one of the greatest stress relievers known. Just be-ing affectionate with someone and feeling a physical and mental closeness with a person you care about can do wonders for your stress levels. Yet it seems, especially in marriages, that having sex gets placed on the bottom of our list of things to do. Some people see it as just another chore to get out of the way.

Because most people's lives move at such an intense speed, we need to schedule in a date night just as we would a doctor's appointment. The idea that romance and making love has to be spontaneous does not fit into most people's lives in this day and age. It is better to schedule it in than not to do it at all.

Over time, a relationship that was once passionate and loving can turn dull and uninteresting if it is not nurtured. If you are stuck in this rut, make a commitment to breathe some life and excitement back into the relationship with your significant other. Make a date with your partner. Get a relative or friend to take the kids for the night and then get dressed up and have a romantic candlelight dinner—at home. Put some soothing music on to play softly in the background so that you can talk to each other. Tell one another what you really like and love about the other person. This is not the time to bring up anything negative, so do not go into all the things you do not like about each other. Act as if you have only known each other for a few weeks. Hold hands and really make an effort to romance your date. Try to reconnect with each other and see where the evening takes you.

One of the true killers of passion is to take work to bed with you, either physically or mentally. No one wants to feel they are competing for attention at such an intimate time. Talking about work before, during, or while you are involved in passionate romance is the kiss of death for intimacy.

Working at It

Having a balanced life takes some creativity, a whole lot of flexibility, and constant determination in order to take control of your life so you can live it to its fullest. Six months from now fill in the percentage guidelines on page 146 again, and compare them to the percentages with which you started. You will see if you have made any progress and can determine which areas still need more work. Just like a tightrope walker who has to constantly adjust his body to stay in balance, you will have to constantly adjust your life to make it work for you.

9

GET A GRIP ON TIME

Did you ever notice that there are some people who seem to get so much more done in less time? They always get things done by or before the deadline. They all have the same amount of time as you do each day at work, yet they seem more efficient and productive. You are still at work, while they are on the way home. You are sitting there stressing while they are already relaxing. What is their secret?

Their secret lies in the exceptional personal habits they have developed over the years. Instead of working longer and harder, they have learned to work smarter. Sure, they have the same challenges as you. But, they have decided that their time is a most precious asset, and have become skilled at using it wisely. They do not squander it away. You too can learn to change your habits. It takes time, practice, and a tenacious resolve to make change, but it is well worth the effort.

Realize that getting a grip on time and getting a grip on stress are inexorably linked. Every time waster you have cuts down on your productivity, and causes tension and stress. Every bad habit you continue with only makes your day miserable. As bad days grow in length and number, you may be putting yourself on that road to burnout. It is time to take control of your time. I am not saying this is a cakewalk, but you can do it.

TRACKING YOUR TIME

Do you know what your biggest time consumers are? Do you know where your time goes each day? Most people have no real clue, although they think they do. One of the most effective ways to see how time is wasted is to keep a time log, sometimes referred to as time diary or activity log. I know what you are thinking; I do not have time. Make the time! You need the feedback. You must know how your time is being spent before you can effectively create change.

Whenever I ask seminar participants for a show of hands of how many have tried this, I get very few responses. When I ask those who respond how it helped them, they give a great testimonial on how effective it is. They always agree that the feedback the log gives them helps them to make changes. One participant stated it was a real eye opener because he did not realize how much time he spent doing tasks that did not achieve his goals. Others have stated it helps them to identify those constant annoying interruptions. A time log shows you patterns of behavior that you must change, and it also shows you patterns of behavior that you must discuss with others, in order to help you be more efficient.

In one of my recent seminars for a government agency, a young manager, under 30 years old, showed me how he kept his time log on a PDA for two weeks. It was short, yet effective. He actually kept track of every minute, and said it was one of the most productive uses of his time he ever spent. A discussion followed with other participants as to whether it was better to use paper or a PDA. It does not matter. Use what works for you. I do suggest you keep the record as the day actually unfolds because you will never remember it in detail hours later. Some of the time-wasting events that transpired or some of the things you accomplished will be forgotten or omitted.

Keep It Simple

This does not have to be an elaborate log. (See Figure 9.1.) As you go throughout the workday, jot down what you did, who was involved, and the real time you spent on it. Also list any interruptions, time wasters, and stress breaks that occur. Rate yourself (e.g., 1 to 5) as to whether you felt you were accomplishing the task or goal. This gives you a realistic picture of whether you are getting the right things done in the right manner.

Make it short, specific, and anecdotal, but do not leave anything out. You want to capture the big picture of how an entire day is spent over a period of time. Do this for a period

FIGURE 9.1   Time Log

Activity, Task, Project	Date, Time	With Whom	Rate Your Accomplishment
Strategic planning meeting	Mon., 9–11:30	Senior management	2/Not done yet.
Association lunch meeting	11:30–2:00	Association board	3/Planned convention.
Interrupted by delivery problem	2:00–3:30	My staff	5/Solved it.
Employee interviews	3:30–5:30	Applicants	4/Hired one of four, two needed.
Filed papers, created to-do list	5:30–6:00	Self	5/Done.
(Note: Rating scale shows the higher the number the higher the rate of accomplishment.)			

of one to two weeks, or however long it takes to give you an overview of your days. This gives you a look at how and where you spent your time, how productive you were, and what or who wasted your time. You can also get an idea of how you use your personal and family time. The log helps you to realize how much time you spend destressing, or with your family.

After you have kept this diary for one or two weeks, go back and analyze it. Ask yourself the following questions about each day:

- Did I get my top priorities done?
- Which events prevented me from completing my priorities?
- Who or what were the biggest interruptions? How can I eliminate them?
- What kind of unexpected emergencies or crises popped up?
- What can I do to prevent these time wasters from happening again?
- What else can I do to become more efficient and productive?

Carefully assess your log and look for certain tendencies. Investigate which events keep happening again and again to discover who or what is wasting your time. Decide which activities need to be added, eliminated, or changed.

IF YOU FAIL TO PLAN, YOU PLAN TO FAIL

To-do lists have been around forever. What I find interesting is the number of people who create them and do not use them. They tell me that there are too many emergencies and fires popping up, so they are thrown off their plan. There is a good reason for this. They are constantly dealing with urgent matters because they have not learned to do the tasks and items ahead of time that prevent things from blowing up in their face. Procrastination makes urgency your constant companion.

There are also events that happen, no matter how much planning you do, that are going to be both urgent and important. Crises will pop up. When they happen, react quickly and calmly. Get others involved who are critical to the issue. Delegate what you were working on, or put it temporarily aside.

One of the best ways to prevent future fires is to conduct fire drills. That means creating detailed plans for possible negative situations or worst-case scenarios. If you are a manager, train all employees in these areas, and be sure they are ready to deal with them in the future. Use past crises as a basis for training, making sure mistakes are not repeated.

Flexibility Is Key

Some people are simply unrealistic, trying to accomplish too much in one day. Their list becomes a fantasy of an ideal day, leaving no time for any flexibility. A list must be fluid to reflect the realities of the day. Stuff happens and priorities change as the day unfolds. You have to be ready for all possibilities. Sometimes the list has to be scrapped altogether. Other times, tasks take longer than you realized. You must also allow time for breaks and some stress reduction, as working nonstop is not healthy. Do not make a list that has so much on it that you accomplish very little, because you will leave work feeling stressed and guilty.

Look at goals and items to be accomplished from a macroview at first. Look at the big picture. If you have sat down at the beginning of a year or quarter and set goals, then you have a sense of direction. That advanced planning creates a set of monthly goals, tasks, and projects. It should give you a master list from which to work. From that list comes your weekly and daily plans.

How to Prioritize

When creating your daily slate of items, list items to be completed that are both urgent and important. These are your priorities. In other words, these are so important that if you do not do them, eventually you may lose your job or will be out of business or some other critical negative consequence may happen. Rank them any way that works for you. For example, label them A-1, A-2, A-3, B-1, B-2, B-3, and so on, or simply 1 through 5 or 10. Estimate the approximate time you think it will take to complete the task plus a little extra time. After these are finished, then work on those items that are important, but not yet urgent. In other words, you are working on them before they become an emergency or disaster. You are getting these tasks and activities done so you do not have to put out fires and be constantly stressed. Stay away from useless meetings and interruptions, because although those tasks may be urgent, but not important, they often fool you into placing them as a high priority.

Items that are not urgent and not important are of the lowest priority and value, and are best left undone. Some people spend a lot of time in the evening doing trivial, low-value activities because they are exhausted from putting out fires all day. If this is you, beginning a stress-reduction program becomes both urgent and important, otherwise you will be a perfect candidate for burnout.

GETTING LOOSE FROM TIME ABUSE

Interruptions are unavoidable and everyone has to deal with them. Whether you are interrupted by phone or by visitors, it is part of life. Some people do not mind the interruptions because it gives them a break from the task at hand. Others do not want people to dislike them, so they allow people to walk in and visit. Interruptions wanted or unwanted eat away at your time.

But face it, there are people who have no respect for your time and never will. They come by and barge in with some trivial urgency or something that is important to only them. Sometimes they just drop in to socialize. Sometimes your subordinate complains about not being able to accomplish a task, so he dumps it on you. You take care of the problem, either because you think that is what a good boss should do, or you do not want him to do a bad job.

The result is still the same: time wasted from working on your priorities. There are times when you just have to draw the line and let people know you cannot be interrupted, or you cannot take on more responsibilities because you are already overloaded.

Rearrange the Place

We can and must take some precautions to prevent interruptions from destroying our productivity. One of the reasons we frequently get interrupted is because we create a work area that is conducive to interruptions. We set up our desk area in a manner that invites people in to chat. If you work behind a desk, look at the location and direction it faces. If people can see you, they will stop and talk. Turn the desk away from the door or opening, or hide it from view altogether.

If possible, let people know when you are available. Have specific times when you have an open door policy. Let them know that when the door is closed, you are in an important meeting, or are working on something difficult or involved, and do not want to be disturbed. You can create a fun sign on the door such as, "Going insane, come back in an hour" or "Imprisoned by a project, see me when I'm paroled." Do not take phone calls during this time. Later sort calls, and return them according to priority.

Be Proactive

When people stop in, and you are working toward a deadline, get up and walk over to the door to talk with them. They will get the message. Set up a meeting for a later time. Another way to discourage people from stopping or staying long is to remove all the chairs from the office. One manager has told me that he keeps folding chairs, folded up and hidden from view, and it discourages visitors from staying very long. You want to send the message that your time is valuable and you cannot waste it. Most people will realize that you are not being rude, just productive. You want people to respect your time. One more item you may have not thought of: If you keep a jar of candy on your desk, hide it. It acts like a magnet and draws people into your office.

One operations manager told me that he has a big desk clock, and when people walk in, he lets them know how much time they have, and turns the clock toward them. They usually finish before the time runs out. He told me he has earned the nickname, "the clock man," but now people respect his time.

Of course, there is the old trick that many have used of having your assistant call you on the phone to tell you that there is an important call, or you have a meeting to attend. Many have used this to get away from a chronic interrupter or unwanted vendor. That can only work so many times before people figure it out, and start to think you are rude.

If you are in a management position and staff members come to you with a problem to solve, there is a simple solution. Tell them you would be glad to help them, but only after they have come with a potential solution to the problem. Tell them to get suggestions from others. They will have to think about it for a while before they jump up and run to you for help. They often come up with a solution before they burden you with the problem.

Technology Can Hinder or Help

With the advent of cell phones and pagers in the past 10 years, people can contact us 24 hours a day. That is one of the reasons we work when we are in cars or are at home. Technology takes us away from a balanced life. You may want to consider changing your cell phone number, and giving it to a few select people. Think about how many people have your phone number. Are they constantly interrupting you at all times, making you reactive to situations? You must realize that you cannot work on your number one priority because you are always taking these calls, and often putting out fires.

One of the best pieces of technology to enhance productivity is a telephone headset. If you spend huge amounts of time on the phone, and do not have a headset, you probably go home with a stiff neck and a headache. Not only does it allow you to multitask, but it enables you to stand up, stretch, and destress while talking. I have one with a very long cord that enables me to move around my office while talking. It keeps my energy up, and makes me sound more alive to the other party.

PERKIES VERSUS GRUMPIES

We all have peak energy times. Many people have more energy in the morning, just after they get up. I like to call these people perkies. Others claim they are not early morning people and have more energy as the day goes on. I like to call these people grumpies. Others like to stay up late at night. Determine which is your highest energy period, and when you are most alert. This is the time to reserve for doing difficult projects and tasks that take the greatest thinking and creativity.

Do not get caught up in the time trap of doing only the things you like when you have the most energy. People tell me they can work faster that way, and get all the easier and pleasant tasks out the way. You wind up putting off the most difficult and unpleasant tasks, and get caught up in the procrastination zone.

PROCRASTINATION:
THE SABOTEUR OF SUCCESS

Have you ever analyzed why you procrastinate? You probably have put off thinking about it. I have come to the conclusion that it is normal human nature to put off anything we are afraid to do. Sometimes we are afraid to do a task because it seems so overwhelmingly huge, difficult to understand, or we fear making mistakes. Especially if you are a perfectionist, you may have trouble getting started, as you want to make sure what you do is just right.

Many people procrastinate because they just do not like doing certain tasks or projects. It is either unpleasant, monotonous, difficult, or very involved, so they tend to do the things they enjoy before the things they dislike. They do the easier things first, putting off the most difficult things, as if there is some magical time when they will enjoy it more. Remember: If you never start, you will never finish!

How to Put off Procrastination

There are many things we have to do in life we do not enjoy, but that is part of being successful. There is an old adage that has become a mantra of mine for many years, and has had a great impact on many of my seminar participants. It says, "Winners do all the things that losers hate to do." I do not know who said it first, but is an irrefutable truth. It will be unpleasant whether you do it now or later. But if you do it now, you will be rewarded by having less pressure and stress on you.

People frequently tell me that they save things for the last minute because they work better under pressure. Some say it gives them a rush. Research shows you do not work better, you just work faster. By working faster, you tend to make more errors, or you do not have a finished product that is your best work. Then you have to fix the mistakes, or risk being told by your boss that the project was not good enough, creating more stress.

Positive self-talk is critical to overcoming procrastination. You have to pump yourself up to get unpleasant things done. Tell yourself over and over, "Get started now" or "Get it done" to help you to get going. Once you get started, keep at it until you have finished a large piece of it or all of it.

If the project is very involved, create a list of all the tasks and activities involved and prioritize them. Sometimes it is good to break the project or task down into smaller chunks, doing a little each day. If you do not have that luxury, then take on the hardest part first. The rest will seem easier. Work on that piece when you have the most energy and your mind is most awake. If that does not work, try an easier part that will motivate you to continue. Set a deadline date or time for yourself, and keep going at it to meet that deadline. Those people who manage their time well do not let anything interfere with the deadline they set. Always take breaks to stretch, exercise, or meditate. When you are done, reward yourself. I fully expect to take a nice vacation when I finish this book.

CLEANING UP STUFF

In my time management seminars, I always begin discussing the topic of paper and clutter by asking a few poignant questions. I start off with, "How many have not seen the surface of your desk in months because of the piles of paper and clutter?" The majority of attendees raise their hand. Next I ask, "How many of you have piles of paper on the floor, all over your office or cubicle?" Again, over half raise their hands. Finally I ask, "How many of you take stuff home, and have continued the piles in your house, because you ran out of room at work?" I am stunned and amazed at how many people raise their hands, all sheepishly smiling and laughing. I have had people tell me that any flat surface is fair game.

Finally, I ask them to write down a good reason why they must have all those papers strewn about in piles. Nobody ever does, although some insist they know what is in each pile. To them, it is like organized chaos. But when I begin to explain the absurdity and danger of the piles, they begin to realize how they conned themselves into believing this is an effective way to organize their paperwork. You must get a grip on clutter!

A Major Distraction

I guarantee that you have saved many different paper items that are not needed. You could probably deep six from 25 to 50 percent of the paper items you have in those piles and never miss them. Having less paper really is better. Having empty space is really all right. Make the garbage can and a shredder your best office friends.

All those piles of papers on the desk and floor are a major distraction. They keep you from being focused on the immediate priority you must finish. Think of each pile sitting there, calling to you saying, "Look at me," "Here I am," "Work on me next." Since you can only work on one task or pile at one time, start cleaning them up. Do not let them take you away from doing the things that are critical to keeping your job or running your business.

One of our biggest time wasters is looking for misplaced papers and folders. The anger and frustration that comes with looking for something misplaced only leads to more stress in our workday. Having all those piles only ensures that we will misplace things. You must get in the habit of filing papers away or throwing them out. Ask yourself the following:

- How old is it? Is it too old to be relevant today?
- When was the approximate last date I used it?
- What are the chances I will ever need it again?
- If I need it again, can I re-create or research the information?

How to Shrink the Paper Tiger

There are basically only three things you can do with paper, whether old or new. You can act or work on it now, which includes delegation, you can file it in a logical, labeled place for later, or you can chuck it. No, there is no other category, such as I'll think about it for a while, or put it on the edge of my desk and come back to it a little later.

Learn to get a grip on your desktop. Start working on the piles on your desk first, as they are probably the most important papers. Eliminate them, by placing them in one of the three categories we discussed. Keep your desk clean so that you have in front of you only that top priority task or project on which you are working. You will feel so much better with a clean desk. At the end of each day, clean off your desk before you leave. Place tomorrow's number one priority out so that you can start on it the next day. Clean, sort, and file during your low energy periods, or times when the mental juices are not flowing.

Get an efficient filing system, one that allows you to retrieve items quickly. In order for your system to work, you need to file things away at least on a weekly basis. Otherwise, it becomes overwhelming, and we start more piles. After you clean your desk, start working on those floor piles.

Use files with broad categories. You can file alphabetically, chronologically, by colors, or by whatever way works for your situation. The trick is to have a system that is easy for you to use, as well as any other staff members who must access the files. On each file folder list the names of items or types of items you have placed in that folder. At the very beginning of that file drawer, place an alphabetical list of all the files in that drawer. It's a lot easier to look at a list than to finger through each file. This at least assures that you are in the right drawer. When a file folder is removed, have people write down who removed it and when. Otherwise, you will spend hours hunting down missing files.

We all get too much mail. If you have an assistant who can screen the mail and pass on only the important items, you are going to save time. Find a time of day to sort through your mail when you have lower energy. Many people tell me they sort mail while on hold on the phone or while faxing something. Most of it does not require you to think very hard. If you must respond to something that requires creative thinking, do it at your peak time when you have more energy. Add new appointments from correspondence immediately into your calendar. Skim magazines, and cut out articles of importance, and file them for when you may need them. This keeps you from creating piles of magazines on the floor.

Many people continue their bad habits into their personal lives, not putting stuff away, and living lives of stepping around clutter. Some people are addicted to buying, and are obsessed with collecting a lot of stuff. They keep things forever, afraid to get rid of it because it cost money. If you have not used personal items at home in years, why are you keeping them? I will bet some of it is so old, it can go into the Smithsonian. Make a commitment to get busy cleaning clutter and throwing out all the stuff you have not used and will never use. Start slow, and do a little each day or week. Less clutter at home means less tension in your life.

MEETING MADNESS

We have all spent countless hours in useless meetings. For many people, meetings are a place where minutes are kept and hours are wasted. If you are in a position to run the meetings, ask yourself if the meeting is really necessary. Can an email or phone call work just as well? I have seen so many departments and companies hold meetings every Monday morning just for the sake of holding a meeting. There is no firm purpose or real need, and whoever is leading the meeting just wings it with no agenda. Meet only when it is really needed. If you must call a meeting, think through what you are trying to accomplish and the minimum number of people that must attend. Do not invite people who have no reason to be there and waste their time. If you are asked to attend, and it does not concern you, ask to be excused.

Preplanning Is the Key

Create an agenda of specific issues you will cover, along with a specific time allotted for each item. As mentioned in Chapter 7, allot time for a little fun before the meeting starts, especially if it is going to require some creativity and tough decisions. The laughter will relax people and get their creative juices flowing.

Allow others to lead the discussion on certain items with which they are more familiar. Take some of the responsibility off yourself and delegate it to others. Have the agenda passed out to all attendees in advance so they come prepared. Put the agenda up on a sheet of flip chart paper for all to see. Have someone take notes, and type up those notes and give them to all attendees within 24 hours. Be very specific in the notes about who is responsible for any follow-up action along with any deadlines.

Start and end your meetings on time. If someone is late, do not wait for them, or repeat what you already said. All you are doing is rewarding bad behavior, and punishing those who are on time. Some managers have told me they take all the chairs out of the room once the meeting starts. Those who show up late must stand for the meeting.

Some organizations, that like having fun, actually make people who are late wear a dunce hat or something silly, or sit them in a corner, or make them pay a fine. Keep it light and funny, but never humiliating! Consider having the late person be responsible for getting the notes typed up and passed out afterward. Let people know you are serious about the way you run a meeting, and they will get serious about attending

To keep the meeting moving along, you may want to consider meeting without chairs, especially if it is a short meeting. Many people have told me that this really helps their meetings to be more productive, and they end much sooner. Do not get sidetracked by interruptions. Put a "Do Not Disturb" sign outside the door, and stick to the items on the agenda. Appoint someone as a parliamentarian to keep the meeting on track.

FIGURE 9.2   Time Management Quiz

Take the following time management quiz to determine whether you need to change your habits and practices. Begin monitoring your day and making changes for all those to which you answered no.

	Yes	No
I make a conscious effort to manage my time every day.	___	___
I monitor my habits with a time log once a year.	___	___
I plan and schedule every day, as best I can.	___	___
I set goals and stick to them, until accomplished.	___	___
I prioritize important items before they become a crisis.	___	___
I am good at dealing with interruptions.	___	___
I know how to say no when needed.	___	___
I attend only necessary meetings.	___	___
I am able to find some quiet time when needed.	___	___
I give my cell phone number only to a chosen few.	___	___
I use technology to make me more productive.	___	___
I use my high-energy times for difficult tasks.	___	___
I do not procrastinate.	___	___
I delegate when needed (if applicable).	___	___
I clean my desk every night before I leave.	___	___
I know where to find anything I need.	___	___
I throw unneeded items away immediately.	___	___
I am not a perfectionist.	___	___
I do not waste other people's time.	___	___
I take stress breaks when needed.	___	___

Managing your time means managing your stress. (See Figure 9.2.) The two go hand in hand. You have been given ideas and tips to cut corners and work more efficiently. You can make the commitment and do the things you do not like to do, or you can sit back and keep the same habits, and of course nothing will change. As Yogi Berra once said, "If you don't set goals, you can't regret not reaching them." The choice is yours.

10

Fifty Ways to Leave Your Stressors

1. Find Some Downtime at Work

If you spend every minute of your day working and never taking a break, you will eventually wear down or even burn out. Make sure you do take all the breaks that are allowed at work. Get up, move around, and get the blood flowing. Or, if you have begun meditating, practice a minimeditation to lower stress.

It is best not to eat lunch and work at the same time. Stretch, exercise, or meditate before you eat. If you can, get away from your desk or work area. A change of scenery can do wonders. If there is a lunch room or cafeteria, sit down and chat with others and try to find something upbeat or funny to discuss. Stay away from negative people. If you prefer to eat at your desk and you have an office, try lowering the lights and playing soft music.

2. Stay Away from Office Politics

Humans are political animals, and workplaces are political zoos. Certain friendships and alliances develop, and conflicts often result due to loyalties to one another. Competing and jockeying for position and power is natural, and it can bring out the worst in people. Minor disagreements and frictions can frequently escalate into major conflicts and all-out battles. Stay clear from as many of these hassles as you can. They are not worth the stress they create. Know when to stand firm or take action that will protect your job. When you cannot avoid these situations, use positive politics, employing assertiveness with wisdom and tact.

3. Avoid the Grapevine

Every workplace has its own invisible form of communication that spreads information, rumors, and innuendo. Sometimes the information is correct, but the problem lies in the fact that we often do not know what is fact or fiction. When there is a vacuum of official communication, the grapevine fills the void, often with incorrect or negative information. People will make up information, especially if they have their own agendas. Unfortunately, negative news tends to travel faster, and often becomes worse than it actually is, breeding fear, anger, and stress.

Do not believe in news spread via the grapevine because rumors, gossip, and misinformation can only add to your stress. The grapevine is famous for decreasing productivity, and it prevents you from focusing on the task at hand. It results in more worrying and tension than you need. Tell yourself you will not let negative rumors erode your morale or motivation until you learn the real truth.

4. Deal with Change Better

The philosopher Heraclitus stated, "Nothing endures but change." Change is constant, unpredictable, yet inevitable. People do not take to change very well. We like the status quo and fear change. When change is coming at work, you have three choices in dealing with it: You can fight it, you can accept it and live with it, or you can look for a new job or career. Change can be positive, and serve as a catalyst for a significant life-changing move.

Realize that resistance to change is a common and natural reaction. But if change is coming, do not fight what is uncontrollable. It is a waste of energy and time. If you decide to accept the change, you must change your own expectations about the way things will be in the future. Next, you need to get busy and stay focused. In order to transition into the new situation, you need to gather information and talk with a lot of people. Do not be afraid to ask for help. The more you know, the better you deal with the change, and how it will impact you. Look for the positive opportunities that exist for you in the changes ahead.

5. Watch What You Say to Yourself

Our thought processes are critical to the way we respond to stress. We are constantly thinking about events that happened or imagining what may happen. At the same time, we have an endless inner commentary of self-talk, making judgments and statements about those events. Many times we are unaware of this ongoing conversation with ourselves, but that self-discussion determines how we react, and how stressed we feel.

Be aware of your negative thinking. Listen for the negative phrases that you are saying and thinking. As soon as you think or hear yourself saying a negative, stop! Change that negative thought or phrase into a positive, and restate it to yourself. This process is known as reframing. You are writing a new script for the event. You are looking for the positive in the event or situation; at least try to make it less negative. With a little practice, you will be amazed at how easily you can change your thought processes. After a while, you will find that you will not allow the negatives to creep in.

Of course, no one can be positive or think happy thoughts all the time. When you cannot, the trick is to get away from the negative, and try to put yourself in a neutral frame of mind. Reinforce this process with the habit of using positive affirmations, and you will deal with stress much better. Tell yourself, "I can handle this," "It is not that bad," or "Everything will eventually be okay."

6. Do a Plus-Minus Analysis

This idea comes from my sales training seminars. It helps salespeople to close the sale when they are sitting face to face with a prospect. I ask people to draw a line down the middle of a sheet of paper. Ask the prospect all the positive reasons for buying versus all the negative reasons for not buying. If you sold the clients on the benefits and value you offer, the positive list is always greater. This helps them to make the buying decision.

Many times in life we need to do the same kind of analysis of situations we face. This technique will help you to make a decision about continuing in a difficult situation. If your job has reached the point where you are experiencing severe stress everyday, and are on the road to burnout, then you must thoroughly assess the advantages and benefits of staying in that job. Draw a line down a piece of paper, and list the advantages and disadvantages, or the pluses and minuses. If the minuses far outweigh the pluses or benefits, then it may be time to make a job or career change. Doing a plus-minus analysis can be a real catalyst for making change.

7. Do Not Bring It Home

Do you bring your work home, either literally or figuratively? Finishing something at home on occasion is okay, but to bring work home constantly is not good for you or your loved ones. Bringing work home in your mind, and being in another world, thinking about it all night, does not let you destress. Try a mini-meditation to clear your mind.

8. Find Some Downtime to Relax at Home

When you get home, there are probably family issues and chores with which you have to deal. Often times, these compound your stress from the workday. As soon as you walk in the door, give yourself a chance to decompress. Let your family know that you need a time-out with some alone time. Pick one of the many ways we discussed earlier and use it to lower the stress and reenergize. Then you will be able to handle domestic issues much better. Find a second time to destress just before bedtime. A hot bath and a good book, with soft music, can help you to sleep.

9. Turn Off the TV

So many people spend time after work dozing off in front of the TV. In order to recharge, eliminate some of the TV time. To have a thriving life, you have to make the time to destress. Time has got to come from somewhere. Start keeping a log of how many hours of TV you watch. You just might be shocked. This is time you could be doing something you enjoy, that relaxes you, like exercising or spending time with the kids.

I am not anti-TV, but there are so many mindless reality shows and sitcoms that add nothing to your life. There are many 24-hour news channels spilling out the same news over and over again. You only need to see those stories once. Much of the news is negative and many of the drama shows are filled with violence. This does not do anything to lessen stress. If you are going to watch TV, make it a program that is either educational or fun, and creates a diversion for your mind. Search for informative channels that give you a new learning experience.

10. Count Your Blessings Every Day

So many people start and end their day looking at how bad things are for them. Is this you? If so, you need to change the way you look at life. It truly is better to look at events through rose-colored glasses. Start each morning telling yourself (and God) how grateful and thankful you are for another day. Focus on the positives that are in your life. It is all about perception. Be thankful for all the things you love and appreciate, such as friends, family, your health, and your talents. If you focus on the negatives in life, or make everything negative, then your whole outlook and the way you react to stress will be negative.

Consider writing out a list of all the positives in your life. Start each day by looking at that list and realizing how thankful you are for these blessings. Keep a blessings diary and at the end of each day, just before going to sleep, write down all the positive things about living on that day. The blessing can be as simple as: I had a wonderful hot shower in the morning.

11. Do Not Sweat the Petty Stuff

Many people take an event and focus on the negative threat of that event, making it a stressor. They catastrophize, awfulize, and look at things with a warped point of view. They whine about the should be's. Small things will go wrong every day. Do not blow difficult situations out of proportion. Do not distort your perception of events. They are almost never as bad as you imagine. If something happened once, it does not mean it will happen again, or it will always be that way. If you spend too much energy on the small stressors, you will have none left for the major stressors, and you will not be able to cope with the truly difficult and stressful situations that come your way.

12. Rituals versus Change

A ritual is simply a procedure that you do again and again, the same way every time. Rituals can help us if we are under constant stress, because they give us a feeling of familiarity and comfort. Getting up the same time every day, getting ready for work in the same manner, and going to work the same way each day can save time, and make us feel in control. We are better able to predict how events will unfold. Before going to bed, try setting out clothing and items you need for work for the next day. This organization will help you to sleep better and a little later.

As calming as rituals can be, some people find excitement in mixing up the system. They do not want to feel like an automaton, doing the same thing, the same way every day. They seek out different practices. For example, if they drive in to work, they may look for alternative routes for a change of scenery. They may stop at a different coffee shop along the way. If they exercise by walking, they are always looking for a new park or outdoor spot that will give them a sense of excitement. Decide whether ritual or change helps you to handle stress better, and go with it. I personally like a blend of the two. I need a change once in a while or life gets a little dull.

13. Get a Thorough Exam

Previously, we looked at all the symptoms of burnout and stress. Sometimes these symptoms are so frequent that they hide the real symptoms of something else that may be lurking in the background. Exhaustion or change in appetite, while these symptoms are signs of stress, can also be indicative of something far more serious. Getting a complete physical exam from your physician can eliminate hidden conditions before they become more serious. When I get an annual exam, I get a complete blood workup and analysis, in order to be sure everything is normal. It gives me peace of mind.

Unfortunately, many people get an exam only when symptoms become chronic and acute, so often it is too late. Men, in particular, hate to see a proctologist. Some women hate to go for gynecological exams and mammograms. If you think something is not right, trust your instincts and go to the doctor. You will eliminate the stress that you put on yourself from worrying about the "what if's" and from not knowing.

Many people do not seek psychological help when they need it for a variety of reasons. Depression and burnout that come from stress must be addressed before they become chronic. If you are experiencing changes in your behavior and the way you cope with stress, you need to get a grip. Sudden changes in eating and drinking habits, or the use of drugs, are a clear indication that you need help.

14. Get Enough Sleep

Most research shows that we need seven or eight hours of sleep a night to function at peak performance. Sleep enables you to relax and recharge and it helps to combat stress. If you want to sleep well, eliminate those substances that keep you awake such as alcohol, caffeine, and cigarettes. Drinking more than two alcoholic beverages, while helping you to fall asleep quicker, has the opposite impact in the middle of the night. It wakes us up very early, and prevents us from getting back to sleep. Remember that caffeine is found not just in coffee, but also in tea, soda, and chocolate.

Very heavy meals should be finished at least three hours before bedtime if you want to sleep through the night. Consuming large meals, very late, stresses our digestive system, and can give us very vivid, and often unpleasant dreams that can wake us up.

Avoid naps during the day, unless they are very early. Sleep that you get during the day just prevents you from sleeping at night. If you must nap, anything longer than 30 minutes can have a negative impact on your sleep cycle. Also avoid late night, strenuous exercise because the flow of oxygen to the cells reenergizes you and keeps you awake longer. If you need to destress, take a more leisurely walk in the early evening. It can act as a catalyst for sleep.

What you do immediately before you go to bed has a great impact on how you sleep. The key is to do something that calms and relaxes you. If you are going to read, make it something light, upbeat, and fun. The same goes for movies you watch. Watching concerts before going to bed affects some people because they hear the music over and over again in their heads, and it prevents them from falling asleep.

As I mentioned in Chapter 4, meditation is a wonderful way to calm the mind before going to sleep. Positive affirmations at this time are very helpful. Try taking a warm bath to help induce sleepiness. Finally, avoid family conflicts or arguments just before bedtime.

15. Learn to Manage Your Anger

Anger is a natural reaction to certain situations and events. Anger also has a positive side to it, because anger can also motivate us to be proactive, and take charge of things. Unfortunately, many people don't know how to express their anger properly, so they keep it bottled up, fermenting inside. Others are fearful that they will erupt in rage or become violent. Still others become enraged frequently, often because of something as trivial as having to stop at a red light. Anger has a destructive impact on your overall health. Anger has a shattering impact on relationships, whether it is at work with your peers or at home with your loved ones. Much research shows that people who are angry all the time are more prone to heart attacks and tend to die younger. The key is to learn how to manage your anger the correct way.

When there is conflict that causes anger, whether it is at work or home, you have to learn how to resolve it. Keeping the anger inside, or not resolving difficult situations, can only create more stress and resentment. Discussing disagreements and friction with others helps to resolve the situation, so we do not have ongoing strife, hostility, and stress boiling up.

Do you remember the ways of coping that have already been discussed? You hold the key to the level of anger you will have, and how long you will hold on to it. Filling yourself with positive self-talk enables you to cope better, and lowers your degree of anger. Tell yourself, "I am in control," or "I refuse to become enraged." Reframe events in a more positive light. Deep breathing, as discussed in previous chapters, is also a great remedy. Once you have calmed down, you will be able to better think the situation through and resolve it. Remember that the anger only gets in your way and blocks you from working things out.

16. Hang Out with Positive People

Who we have as our friends speaks volumes for who we are. Friends and relationships are important because they give us social interaction and keep us grounded, but, relationships take time and energy. If you are going to have close friendships, it might as well be with positive people.

Many years ago, my wife and I had a few negative friends who were so emotionally draining that we were often mentally exhausted after talking with them. Their life was one crisis after another. They made all the wrong choices in life, and then could not cope with the results. For them, everything was tarnished by seeing events through a dark prism. They constantly complained and were negative about even the good things in their lives. These people would do nothing to help themselves and unknowingly tried to bring us down to their negative level. Being around them was not a joy. They gave nothing positive to our friendships. For our peace of mind and stress levels, we decided to end the friendships. Were we cold and unfeeling? No, we realized we could not help these friends, and they were only making our lives stressful for trying.

People are like chameleons, as we take on the colors of those around us. Develop relationships with positive, optimistic people, who are loving and caring. Seek out people who see life as a positive experience, rather than as something that just happens to them. Spend time with people who will listen to you when you deal with strife, and can give you good positive feedback and advice. Be around those who make you feel that it is great to be alive, because it is.

17. Share Problems with Others

When we are really stressed, and events in life are not going well, we all need the help of others. Some people make the mistake of withdrawing at times like this. My friend, Ron, has had a rough time staying employed because he works in the high-tech field. When things are really bad, he withdraws from others so I may not hear from him for months at a time.

We all need friends and relatives we can lean on from time to time. When life is difficult, we need to seek support and feedback from those we love and respect. Just talking things out (and maybe having a good cry) can be a great aid in getting us back on track. By doing this, it puts things into perspective; we get another point of view and solutions we may not have thought about.

18. Smile a Lot

The more you smile, the happier you are. A smile also makes others smile in return. Try smiling when you are angry. It is virtually impossible, as smiling relaxes the facial muscles. The yoga masters of India have known this for centuries. The Maharishis are always smiling because they know that smiling long enough can actually change your mood. When you are in a negative mood and are stressed out, try smiling for about 15 minutes. You will notice a distinct upswing in your frame of mind.

19. The Power of Prayer

Prayer is another effective tool you can use in your arsenal of weapons to combat stress. Its physical and emotional benefits are incomparable. A great deal of research backs this up, specifically that done by Duke University and Ohio State University. People who pray are much better able to cope with stress, depression, illness, and injury. Prayer enables people to deal with life's most difficult situations. The amazing power of prayer illustrates that ill people who are prayed for heal faster than those who are not.

Attending places of worship gives people a sense of community. This community can provide strength and support during difficult times. Those with a strong faith are better able to cope during tough times, and they can handle tragedy better. Faith gives people hope and optimism that difficult situations will improve. I think this is due to the love, support, and caring people share with others while at church or synagogue.

20. Keep a Stress Log

Keep a short log of the events that stress you out as you go through the day. On a sheet of paper, briefly list the event or situation that happened, what the cause was, who was involved, and how you reacted to it. (See Figure 10.1.) On a scale of 1 to 5, rate your reactions. Use 1 for very little stress and 5 for a high amount of stress. At the end of the day look back and see which events upset you the most. Was it worth the energy you used up on that stressor? Ask yourself how you could have dealt with it better, and what you would do differently the next time. Some people may think this takes too much time, but the time you spend is well worth it. You need this information to help you make change.

FIGURE 10.1   Stress Log

Date, time	Stressor, cause	My reaction	Rating	(1–5)*

*(Rating is based on highest number being the best reaction.)

21. Write It Out

Getting your feelings on paper can feel like opening a pressure valve, especially if you have trouble expressing feelings to others or you do not have a support system to rely on. Scripting your emotions can be almost as good as talking about them. Being creative and putting your life's events into a short story or poetry can relax you, and bring out the creativity you may possess.

22. Help Others Less Fortunate

It does not matter whether it is a soup kitchen, Habitat for Humanity, a church project to help the needy, or working with abused children, helping others who are less fortunate does wonders for relieving stress. It makes you a stronger, better person.

Get involved and volunteer your time, energy, and skills in the community. You will realize that there are so many others less fortunate than yourself. It shrinks your problems down to reality. Doing this will put things into perspective, and will make you realize that too often we sweat the petty stuff. When we help those in need, and do good deeds, it makes us feel great that we have helped others. Many people report feeling a rush or high during and after the time they spend giving. The love and good feelings you share will make you healthier and happier.

23. Commit Random Acts of Kindness

This is closely related to helping those in need and it has the same positive benefits. When you are out running chores, shopping, or traveling there are times when an opportunity presents itself to help someone for a brief moment. It may be holding a door, allowing another driver to go ahead of you, or helping someone put their luggage in an overhead compartment of a plane. All of these acts make you feel good, and have a positive impact on reducing your stress levels.

24. Get Your House in Order

One of the elements that leads to extra stress in our lives is the clutter we have in our homes. There was probably a time when you first moved into your current home or apartment, and thought that you had a lot of room for your stuff. Over time, you collected more and more stuff, without throwing out the old stuff. As a result, you have a mess with less room. Many of those things you probably have not touched or used in years. Who are you saving the stuff for, and why are you saving it? It is a stress creator when you have to search for something and cannot find it because you have too much junk in the way. Think about all the times you have gotten stressed out over something you could not find. Many times my wife had gotten stressed out because she could not find clothing when she wanted to wear it. Now, she cleans out her clothes closet twice a year.

Stop procrastinating and start organizing your home. Make a commitment to schedule time to organize closets and drawers, and throw old, unused items out or donate them to charity. Draw up a list of which rooms, closets, drawers, and spaces need to be organized. Tackle the worst areas first. As you declutter the toughest areas, it will give you the motivation to continue. When you are done, reward yourself.

25. Bathe It Away

When you are stressed, and your muscles feel tight, there is nothing like a hot bath to relax you, and make you sleepy. You can enhance the bath with candles, low lights, and some soft music. The flickering light of the candle adds to the peaceful mood. Scented candles also help to relax you. This can also serve as a place to meditate and repeat positive affirmations. Try this just before going to bed. It clears the mind and helps you to fall asleep faster.

Buy a showerhead that has different settings. They are wonderful for massaging the neck, shoulders, and back, and getting rid of tension. If you decide to replace a tub, upgrade it with the kind that has water jets. It is just like having a hot whirlpool bath in your tub.

26. Give Your Nose a Workout

This is one that some people laugh at, but it is not that different from using scented candles. Aromatherapy employs the use of essential oils or oils containing aromas that have been extracted from plants. These aromatic extracts are used to promote health, reduce stress, and put the body back in balance. Common oils used include vanilla, lavender, and jasmine. The scents from the oils are directly inhaled.

There are many benefits that have been linked to aromatherapy, some proven and some not. Many people find it truly beneficial in relieving anxiety, tension, and stress. Others have used it to improve certain diseases, injuries, and skin conditions, especially when they are added to bath water. Find the scent or combination of scents you enjoy the most, and try it. Just smelling the pleasant aromas is a mood lifter.

27. Get Rubbed the Right Way

Massage is an effective treatment for combating anxiety, tension, and stress, as it actually reduces many of the stress-induced hormones created during the fight-or-flight syndrome. It is one of the ways to achieve pure relaxation and become more mentally alert. In addition, it is great for alleviating certain types of headaches and chronic pain. Massage is a perfect remedy for reducing the muscle tightness, stiffness, and spasms described in earlier chapters. Like stretching, it aids in improving flexibility and range of motion in our joints. When soft tissue is massaged, it brings more blood supply to the cells in that area, decreasing tenderness and tightness. Massage therapy is also indicated to improve circulation and lower blood pressure.

There are many different types of massages, and they can often be confusing (e.g., Swedish, deep tissue, sports massage). Thirty states and the District of Columbia regulate and license massage therapists. Different therapists have different training and use different techniques. Many use more than one technique. Learn which massage is the kind that will benefit you the most. You may have to try a few professionals before you find the one who is best for you.

Contact the American Massage Therapy Association at www.amtamassage.org to sort out much of the information. They will tell you what to expect during a massage, and help you locate a qualified massage therapist in your area. They will also give you a list of questions to ask a massage therapist to help you choose the one that is right for you.

28. Acupuncture and Acupressure

Acupuncture dates back over 2,000 years to the medical practices taught in ancient China. I have discussed the concept of chi or the universal life force of energy in all of our bodies. Traditional Chinese medicine believes that the chi flows throughout the body in patterns via 14 channels or meridians. Each meridian has points along it, called acupoints, which are related to specific organs. When the flow of chi is blocked or interrupted, the result can be sickness and disease. Acupuncture restores the flow of chi and puts the body back into balance. The most common method of acupuncture entails placing ultra-thin metallic needles into a specific acupoint. The needle is then moved by hand in order to stimulate the flow of energy. The practice is virtually painless.

In Asia, acupuncture has been used for centuries to cure hundreds of illnesses and conditions. Many American and European physicians make use of acupuncture to alleviate pain and nausea. It also helps in withdrawal from alcohol and drugs. The National Institutes of Health have funded many research projects and conferences on acupuncture and its benefits. Many research projects have dealt with the ability of acupuncture to cure muscle tightness, spasms, and pain. People garner a feeling of peace and relaxation afterward.

Developed in China over 4,000 years ago, acupressure is a form of acupuncture without the thin needles. Its purpose is the same. The acupoints are stimulated with the hands in order to relieve stress and reduce pain. Fingers, palms, and knuckles are used to apply pressure on the acupoints and unblock any interruptions in the flow of chi. Once again, balance is restored in the body increasing healing, relaxation, and overall well-being.

29. Day at a Spa

If you can afford it, a day at the spa is the ultimate in relaxation and for destressing the mind and body. Everyone enjoys being pampered and feeling special. If you cannot afford it, try getting just a facial at a spa or at a beauty salon.

30. Start Scrapping

Scrapbooking is one of the most popular things to do these days. It is a wonderful way to collect your memories and it allows you to be as creative as you want to be. After my wife and I vacationed in France, my wife created a scrapbook of the trip with a daily diary of everything we did. Now, when we have had a particularly stressful day, and want to destress, we take out the album and it is as if we have had an instant vacation. We relive those wonderful days again and again. Scrapping can be done with your children, friends, and other relatives. There are even scrapping clubs, so it can be a social activity at the same time. Try doing tribute albums to certain people, and albums of someone's life (even your own).

31. Get Cooking
Cooking has a magical way of getting you to focus your mind on what you are doing. It takes your mind off of your troubles because you have to concentrate at times, and at other times, when you are chopping vegetables, for instance, you just can let your mind relax. You do not have to make food that is elaborate or difficult. If you are just getting started, begin with the simple recipes. You will only get more stressed if you start with a recipe that is too complicated. Many couples cook together. They find it a wonderful way to be together and have fun at the same time. When you are finished you will feel that you have accomplished something, and hopefully have food that is good to eat. Try it. You just may find that you are good at it and have discovered a new hobby.

32. Romantic Candlelight Dinners
This may sound corny, but it works! Creating a mood is especially good for enhancing your relationship with someone you care about. Candles are wonderful for making the mood relaxing, and giving a special atmosphere to a dinner. Communication between people just seems to naturally open up, maybe because we are relaxed, and anything that relaxes us relieves stress.

33. Get to the Root of Your Family
Researching family history has become increasingly popular in recent years. Tracing your family genealogy is a

wonderful and fascinating diversion and it is easier than you think. The Internet has many web sites, and there is software you can buy to help you. Many web sites have a database of names, and all you have to do is type in your family name. Others charge a fee for the service. U.S. Census Bureau records are also a valuable tool in aiding you in your quest. And, for a fee, you can also enlist a professional genealogist to assist you.

34. Get Away for a Day

The benefits of a long vacation are obvious. But, destressing two weeks out of the year is not enough. You have to recharge frequently during the other 50 weeks, too. The solution: Get out of town for a day or two. Schedule weekend vacations and getaways throughout the year.

Taking a one or two day minivacation can do wonders for clearing your head and relaxing the body. A complete change of scenery is exciting and fun. There are plenty of places that you can drive to in three to four hours that you probably have not seen. It helps to loosen the grip that work has on your mind and body. Leave the cell phone and pager off so you don't have the distractions of work while you are gone.

35. Go Local

Find someplace new in your county or city where you have never been. Get a map and check it over for new areas to visit. Where are parks or outdoor areas you have not visited? What public or private institutions have you never visited? Check the weekend section of the paper that lists the local events that are happening, plus all the nightlife. Look in the beginning section of your yellow pages directory. Some list must-see attractions and many local activities you can enjoy. It may also have a description of recreational areas, parks, and hiking trails.

36. Out with the Old, In with the New

We often go through our daily routine, doing the same things every day. Routine is good, as it often can help us to cope better. But, everybody needs a change of pace to make life more exciting and even less stressful. Make a list of things you have not done before, but you have a desire to do. It could be a sport, a hobby, a group to join, but be sure it is totally new. Find the type of information and people or groups that can assist you in achieving this new, fun activity. Pursue it with vigor!

37. Hobbies Are Healthy

Hobbies can almost work like a form of meditation, because they help to slow the mind, clear it of the clutter, and get us to focus on something that is enjoyable. Many people gain relaxation and satisfaction just from working with the hobby, as opposed to creating any concrete results. Others receive achievement from their creativity. Find a hobby that you strayed away from years ago, or seek out a new one that lets you use your mind, hands, and creativity. Challenge your brain with a new activity. Become absorbed in something new and diverting, rather than being self-absorbed and worrying about the next day at work.

I recently unearthed my old stamp collection from when I was a child. What warm memories and pleasant thoughts it brought back! I started really getting involved in it, and found out I had some very old, valuable stamps. It was also fascinating to see how many countries from around the world have changed their names, or do not exist anymore. Go dust off that old hobby and rekindle your interest, or start a new one.

38. Become a Groupie

Being around other people can really take our mind off ourselves. It gives us a chance to focus on others, and at the same time it destresses us. If you are not involved in any types of groups, find one or two with which you have something in common. Research local civic groups, social groups, church groups, or special interest groups like language, hobby, or professional associations. Try creating your own group, and have a rotating dinner each month. For example, find 10 couples who really enjoy gourmet food and a little wine, and have fun.

39. Music Can Soothe Your Soul

Some music has a therapeutic effect on us. If you can listen to the right kinds of soothing music, at work or at home, it will help to lower your stress levels. As many aficionados of classical music know, it is very relaxing. For me personally, I like old jazz, particularly those songs sung by the female divas of yesteryear. New age music is also very effective in creating a tranquil mood.

I use my CD headset almost every night when I am out walking my yellow labrador, Beau. If I am not listening to a motivational CD or tape, I am destressing with relaxing jazz, while getting an aerobic walk, and laughing at the trouble that Beau is trying to get into or out of. I also use music when I am doing chores around the house. The music makes the tasks much more palatable.

40. Read What You Love

As a lover of books, I frequently unwind by going to a bookstore or the library and browsing the shelves. When leafing through books, I'm living in the present moment, not thinking about the past or future. Whether I am searching for or reading a book, I destress because it takes my mind off of my work and my hectic schedule. Besides, I find new information about different subjects, so I am constantly expanding my knowledge base and horizons.

41. Start Gardening

Working outside, getting your hands covered with dirt, and caring for plants has an amazing effect on stress levels. Since I live in South Florida, I get to spend a lot of time in my yard, landscaping, trimming, and pulling weeds. This physical activity gets out my frustrations of the week, and relieves my stress. Many friends, neighbors, and relatives report the same benefits. We find it therapeutic and tranquilizing.

I have a cousin in California who works in the fast-paced, hi-tech industry in a sales and marketing position. He grows prize tomatoes in order to cope with the tension and pressure. My wife has a collection of beautiful, flowering orchids that she nurtures every day. It gives her a soothing feeling to see the flowers that bloom from her tender loving care.

Gardening helps to totally clear your mind, and focus on the task at hand. I can personally attest to the fact that it makes you feel good and relaxes you. It has a healing effect, and you see the results of what you have created with your hands. You do not need a large tract of land. You can grow plants in pots, and also keep some indoors.

42. Sunrise, Sunset

If I am lucky, sometimes when I am driving in traffic, I will catch a sunrise or sunset. When I am tense and stressed from the commute, it is as if God is saying, "I am still here. Stop and appreciate the beauty I have given you." It immediately changes my frame of mind. When I look around at the other drivers, whose faces are all pinched up with aggravation and stress from the traffic, I want to shout, "look what you are missing!" Make the time to see a sunrise or sunset; you will feel like you received a gift from God.

43. Nature Walk, Go to the Park, Picnic, Bike Ride, Hike, Bird Watch

All of these activities will get you out and in touch with the beauty of the world around you. Plus, you can do all of these activities with family and friends. You will get in touch with nature and your loved ones while getting some exercise and fresh air all at the same time. The stress of the week will just seem to melt away.

44. Go Shopping

This is my wife's favorite destressor. She loves to hunt the garage sales and flea markets as much as she loves to shop all the stores. Even if she does not buy anything, shopping makes her acutely aware of the moment she is in, and she forgets any stressful problems in her life for awhile. You get exercise by walking and clear your mind by focusing on something other than your life. It is a wonderful, relaxing diversion. But of course, many of you have already discovered this secret.

45. Go to a Concert, Fair, Festival

Whether it is outdoors or indoors, the atmosphere of crowds of people having a good time is a mood lifter. Listening to live music puts you in the moment, and makes you unwind and relax. All of these are good family activities, and just having fun is a great destressor.

46. Go to a Movie, Play, Museum, Planetarium

Spending a few hours at any of these places can transport you into another world. They are great forms of escape from a high-stress world. Try movies and plays that will relax you. Some movies containing high violence and fast action scenes can make you more tense, so choose carefully. Planetariums can help you see the bigger picture, and put life into a different perspective for you.

47. Invest in Pet Power

Pets have a tremendous ability to relieve our stress. Being around cats, dogs, birds, horses, and other animals is therapeutic. They comfort us and take away loneliness. The stroking and massaging of a pet feels good to the pet and us, but more important, it lowers our anger, anxiety, and stress level. Being connected to a pet gives us something else to focus on, especially when we are under pressure. Pets keep us from thinking about ourselves. There is something about the connection between people and a pet that has to be experienced to be understood. They are always there, with unconditional love, and give you a feeling of caring and being cared about.

Pet behavior can be fascinating to watch. Pets are funny and make us laugh. Although my dog, Beau, is 11 years old, I still laugh as much at his antics as I did when he was a puppy. Watching him play and the enjoyment and laughter that comes with it is almost like taking an instant vacation. If you feel that you don't want the responsibility and cost of a dog or cat, then visit pet stores, go to pet shows, or go horseback riding.

48. Go to a Zoo

Simon and Garfunkel were right when they sang, "It's all happening at the zoo." A visit to the zoo has so many wonderful advantages, especially if it is outdoors. It is fun, entertaining, educational, and you get the opportunity to do a lot of walking. Watching animals and their behaviors is stress relieving. The whole family will enjoy it. It takes your mind away from work, your problems, and yourself.

49. Wash and Wax the Car

Before you laugh at this one, keep an open mind. It may sound like work, but many people find it an enjoyable outlet. You get a sense of accomplishment that makes you feel proud, and driving becomes just a little more enjoyable, even if it is for a short time (until it gets dirty again). The real benefit is in the almost meditative effect it can have because it clears your head. It is also good exercise. I challenge myself to wash and wax the car by a certain period of time so I can make it a physical workout. Sometimes I put on a headset and listen to CDs while I work.

50. Create an Action Plan

Now that you have been given many more ways to get a grip on stress, it is time to take action and create a plan. Write out realistic long and short-term goals. Go after those goals with persistence and determination. It takes time to break the old habits that you have had for years, but you can do it. In the next chapter, we will look how to put it all together and achieve success.

11

GETTING AND
KEEPING YOUR GRIP

Throughout this book, I have frequently mentioned how important it is to set goals, stay on course, and change behaviors. I will end with an explanation of the goal-setting process, and how you can create a step-by-step action plan to get and keep your grip on stress. Regardless of the areas in your life you want to change, the goal-setting process is the same. In this case, the goal I will discuss is the reason why you read this book: to lessen the stress in your life so you can function at your best and make your life better. This is an example of setting a personal goal. You can also use this process to set your workplace and professional goals.

By following these guidelines, you will have an organized process to achieve your goals. You will have a blueprint for success by filling out the action plan. Now, you will be able to get a grip on stress and take control of your life.

SETTING NEW GOALS FOR A THRIVING LIFE

1. Passion and Desire

In order to achieve the goal of less stress in your life, you must have a strong passion and desire to achieve it, and set aside the time to destress. If you feel that you cannot or will not make the time, it will not happen. You must believe in yourself. You must have a strong feeling that you know you can do it.

Having a desire to lessen stress is something we all have. This alone will not move you to achieve that goal. But, how bad is the desire burning in you? Is the desire so strong that you are willing to change old habits? It takes about three weeks of work and determination to change a habit. If you do not make change, will the stress destroy your career and family? You have to be so passionate about it that you are willing to take the time during the day to do the specific exercises and practices mentioned in this book. This means rearranging a typical day and changing your habits of behavior. You must make a commitment. If you have the passion, you will have the persistence and determination it takes to achieve your goal.

2. Be Realistic

You have to be honest with yourself. This means you cannot set unrealistic goals. Set goals that you know are attainable even it takes time, money, and a huge effort. If you set a nonattainable goal, you will give up very quickly, become frustrated and more stressed. For example, say you wanted to lessen stress by exercising one hour per day, but also want to change your diet and lose 40 pounds in the next month. This is setting the bar too high. Yes, you can start exercising and lessen stress. You cannot do it for an hour in the beginning if you are out of shape. You must do it gradually. If you change your eating habits, you may lose 15 to 20 pounds, but not 40 pounds. Set realistic goals and you will be much more successful.

3. Analyze Your Current Status

Take a look at yourself and your life as it is today. Where are you now, at the beginning of your plan, in relation to where you want to be? Keep a stress log, review it, and see how often you are getting stressed, and how you are dealing with it. How much time are you spending each day in actual stress management? What activities and practices are you using to lower your stress? You need a baseline from which to start and chart your course.

4. Visualize the End Result

As discussed in earlier chapters, visualization can be used to lower stress levels. It can also be used in the same way to set your goals. Visualize yourself exercising or meditating and relaxing. See yourself as a more energized person, laughing and enjoying life. Visualize yourself basking in the wonderful benefits of achieving your goal. Use the power of your imagination just before you go to sleep, and just as you arise in the morning, when your subconscious mind is most open to suggestions. Aim for 10 minutes of detailed visualization just as you arise, and 10 minutes just before you retire, every day until you achieve your goal.

5. Set a Realistic Deadline

Goals without deadlines are pure fantasy. Many people believe they are going to achieve something someday. They are always getting ready to get ready. You must set a deadline, because it creates urgency. But, it has to be a realistic deadline. You cannot say you will begin fast walking three miles within two weeks if you are out of shape and your legs are not strong. You cannot think you will be meditating for a 45-minute period within one week. It takes time and practice to achieve that. Set a schedule that is practical depending on your job hours, family obligations, and lifestyle. Give yourself enough time to get there. For example, when I was first asked to write this book, I was asked to complete it in eight months. I knew that was an impossible deadline to meet, due to my speaking and consulting schedule, and life balance imperative. I knew I could achieve it in 10 months, which fit in with all the other goals I had set. I finished this book on time, without becoming stressed out.

6. Look for Barriers, Problems, and Obstacles

If you look back over your life and any goals you have achieved, you will realize there have been challenges that arose along the way. Obstacles pop up that seem to throw a curve in our plan. Yet we always figure out a way around them if we are serious about accomplishing our goals. There will be barriers that get in the way of your finding the time to destress.

A good idea is to brainstorm for problems ahead of time. Ask yourself:

- What potential hurdles may get in the way of achieving my stress-reduction goals?
- What is it about my lifestyle that blocks my ability to achieve my goals?
- What do I need to do to successfully remove that obstacle from my life?

- How can I minimize the impact of that impediment to my goal?

7. Identify Who, What, and How

There are certain people or groups of people who will be helpful to you in achieving your goal. That does not mean they are responsible for your success. That depends only on you. Identify those people or groups who can make it easier for you to succeed. For example, if your goal is to destress by exercising at a gym, you may want to find a buddy to work out with, as it serves to motivate both of you. You may also try a personal trainer. You may need to discuss your time needs with your boss or your family and friends.

Resources are always needed in order to reach any goal. Reaching a goal often requires some new information or some know-how. Identify what you need to know in order to get a grip on stress. If your goal is to learn about meditation, you may want to take a class or seek the services of a personal instructor.

How much time will you need per day? Look at your schedule as it exists now. See if there are blocks of time that you can rearrange. Discover when the best time is to work on getting rid of your stress. Maybe you have a half-hour some days and an hour on others, or, perhaps you only have 15 minutes to spare on some days. Remember what I said in previous chapters: Doing stress-reduction techniques 10 times a day for five minutes can be as effective as a one hour block of time.

You may also need to commit some financial resources to lessening your stress. Gyms, equipment, classes, and personal trainers all cost money. Look at your budget and see what will work for you.

8. Create and Implement a Step-by-Step Plan

If you do not write down a clearly defined goal with a step-by-step plan, you will probably not achieve it. Vaguely written goals will not be attained. Goals that are too rigid are also very difficult to achieve.

There is something psychologically binding about definitively writing out a goal and how you will achieve it. No longer is it just a wish or fantasy; now you have a plan of action. You have a sense of direction. This gives you a road map to achievement. If you do not write out your plan, you will not succeed, or you will not reach the level of achievement you wanted. You will wander around like a person lost in the woods without a compass. To quote Yogi Berra, "If you don't know where you are going, you'll probably wind up someplace else."

I once had a person in a seminar tell me he never wrote down goals. He told me he kept them in his head. I asked him to discuss this further with me during the break. When we talked, he told me he was going to change careers from a technology job and go into the area of sales. I discovered he had vague goals, no deadline, and no plan of action. I took his phone number down. I called him every six months for two years to check on his progress. He has yet to make the change, and I do not believe he ever will.

Start with the macroplan, as I talked about in Chapter 9. Define the long-range goal. Next, break it down into the shorter step-by-step goals. A long-range goal can seem so scary and overwhelming at the start. The short-range goals or steps look easier to achieve, and we are more apt to get started. Keep the short objectives or steps visible on a sheet of paper with the name of the goal on top. Keep it where you can frequently see it. (See Figure 11.1.)

FIGURE 11.1   Your Plan of Action

Answer the following questions to create your plan of action to eliminate a major stressor.

What is the biggest stressor in your life?

What physical or mental symptoms is it creating?

What events or situations are creating the stress?

What have you done so far to eliminate the causes?

Why have you not been successful so far?

What do you need to start doing immediately?

What do you need to stop doing immediately?

Who can help or support you?

What resources will you need?

What obstacles or barriers might get in the way?

List the action steps needed to achieve your stress-related goal.

What is your deadline for achieving success?

How will you check your progress along the way?

How will you know you achieved success?

How will you celebrate your success?

9. Constantly Check Your Progress

As you set out to achieve a new goal, you need to stop along the way and take stock of your progress. Look at how far you have come, and see if you are on course. That is why I believe it is important to keep a minilog of what you do each day to get rid of stress. You can look back over a period of time, see how you started, and how you have built yourself up over time to lessening the stress. Any goal you want to achieve is going to have roadblocks and detours along the way. By looking both backward and forward, and checking your progress, you can self-correct along the way to be sure you are on the right path. Seeing the progress you have made is a real motivator.

10. Celebrate Your Achievements

Whenever you achieve minor goals, celebrate by rewarding yourself in some small way. Go out to dinner with your family or buy yourself a small gift. As we move along the pathway to greater successes, we do not celebrate our small successes enough. Whenever you achieve major results, celebrate by rewarding yourself in a major way. Take a vacation or buy something that you may have never dreamed of owning. Have a party and allow others to join in the celebration.

As you achieve each step of your action plan, take the time to do something fun and memorable. Have a good time. You deserve it. When you have reached the total completion of a goal, then set new, higher standards for the next goal.

THE CHOICE IS YOURS

You have been shown many new ways to lessen the stress in your life. Now comes the hardest part. What will you do after you put this book down? How will you change your life? I can show you how to set your goals, and you can fill out an action plan, but if you do nothing different, nothing will change. If you do not like what stress is doing to you, physically and mentally, then do something about it now. It takes a real commitment to make change, and it takes self-discipline to take action. You hold the key. You have taken the first step by reading this book. Now, use the tools I have given you to get a grip on stress.

REFERENCES

AARP. "Having Fun as We Age: A Survey of Adult Fun Styles." Report prepared by RoperASW, *http://research .aarp.org/il/funstyles_2001_1.html*.

Benson, H. 2000. *The Relaxation Response.* New York: Avon Books.

Cannon, Walter B. 1929. *Bodily Changes in Pain, Hunger, Fear, and Rage*, 2nd ed. New York: Appleton, 27.

Cohen, D., A. Tyrell, & A. Smith. 1991. "Psychological Stress and Susceptibility to the Common Cold." *New England Journal of Medicine* 325, 606–612.

Conrad, C., & D. Diamond. 2003. Unnamed research paper presented at the annual meeting of the Society for Neuroscience. New Orleans, LA. November 12.

Cousins, N. 1979. *Anatomy of an Illness.* New York: W.W. Norton.

Everson, S., J. Lynch, G. Kaplan, T. Lakka, J. Sivenius, & J. Salonen. 2001. "Stress-Induced Blood Pressure Reactivity and Incident Stroke in Middle-Aged Men." *Stroke* 32 (6): 1263–1270.

Godden, R. 1989. *A House with Four Rooms.* New York: William Morrow & Co.

Goetzel, R., D. Anderson, R. Whitmer, R. Ozminkowski, R. Dunn, & J. Wasserman. 1998. "The Relationship between

Modifiable Health Risks and Health Care Expenditures: An Analysis of the Multi-Employer HERO Health Risk and Cost Database." *Journal of Occupational and Environmental Medicine* 40 (10).

Kiecolt-Glaser, J., & R. Glaser. "Mind and Immunity." 1993. In D. Goleman & J. Gurin, eds., *Mind/Body Medicine.* New York: Consumer Report Books, 40–65.

LaFreniere, Ed, ed. 2003. *Attitudes in the American Workplace IX.* North Haven, CT: The Marlin Company.

Lizotte, K., & Barbara Litwak. 1995. *Balancing Work and Family.* New York: Amacom.

Lockwood, N. R. 2003. "Work/Life Balance: Challenges and Solutions." *HR Magazine, Research Quarterly* 48 (6): 1–10.

Matteson, Michael T., & John M. Ivancevich. 1987. *Controlling Work Stress: Effective Human Resource and Management Strategies.* San Francisco: Jossey-Bass, 10, 241.

Moody, R. A. 1978. *Laugh after Laugh: The Healing Power of Humor.* Jacksonville, FL: Headwaters Press, 21.

Noll, Georg, et al. 2002. "Mental Stress Induces Endothelial Dysfunction via Endothelian-A Receptors." *Circulation: Journal of the American Heart Association*, May 20.

Northwestern National Life Insurance Company. 1993. "Fear and Violence in the Workplace: A Survey Documenting the Experience of American Workers." Minneapolis, MN: Northwestern National Life Insurance Company.

Parrott, A. C. 1999. "Does Cigarette Smoking Cause Stress?" *American Psychologist* 54 (10): 817–820.

Perkins, A. 1994. "Saving Money by Reducing Stress." *Harvard Business Review* 72 (6): 12.

Selye, Hans. 1976. *The Stress of Life*, rev. ed. New York: McGraw-Hill, 173–178.

Sillaber, I., G. Rammes, S. Zimmermann, B. Mahal, W. Zieglgaensberger, W. Wurst, F. Holsboer, & R. Spanagel. 2002. "Enhanced and Delayed Stress-Induced Alcohol Drinking in Mice Lacking Functional CRH1 Receptors." *Science* 296 (931).

Stein, J. 2003. Unnamed cover story. *Time* (August 4), 48.

Swift, Ann T., & Bradford Swift. 1994. "Humor Experts Jazz Up the Workplace." *HR Magazine* 39 (3): 72–73.

Veninga, R. L., & J. P. Spradley. 1981. *The Work/Stress Connection: How to Cope with Job Burnout.* Boston/Toronto: Little, Brown, and Company, 36–73.

About the Author

Bob Losyk has been helping organizations and individuals to destress for over 17 years. In constant demand as a consultant, trainer, and speaker, his clients range from Fortune 500 corporations to small businesses, associations, and franchises. As founder and CEO of Innovative Training Solutions, he brings 20 years of professional insight and business savvy to his clients, helping them to become more productive and profitable.

He holds the Certified Speaking Professional designation, the highest earned award given by the National Speakers Association. Bob is a frequent guest lecturer at universities on workplace issues. He is the author of the highly successful book, *Managing a Changing Workforce: Achieving Outstanding Service with Today's Employees* (Workplace Trends Publishing, 2001). His management articles have appeared in hundreds of trade and professional journals and magazines. Bob's opinion has been quoted on the cover of the *Wall Street Journal* and he has appeared on many national TV and radio shows.